# R Programming Fundamentals

Deal with data using various modeling techniques

**Kaelen Medeiros**

**BIRMINGHAM - MUMBAI**

# R Programming Fundamentals

Acquisitions Editors: Aditya Date, Bridget Neale
Content Development Editor: Madhura Bal
Production Coordinator: Ratan Pote


First published: September 2018

Production reference: 2290719


Published by Packt Publishing Ltd.

Livery Place
35 Livery Street
Birmingham
B3 2PB, UK.

ISBN 978-1-78961-299-8

www.packtpub.com

mapt.io

Mapt is an online digital library that gives you full access to over 5,000 books and videos, as well as industry leading tools to help you plan your personal development and advance your career. For more information, please visit our website.

## Why Subscribe?

- Spend less time learning and more time coding with practical eBooks and Videos from over 4,000 industry professionals

- Improve your learning with Skill Plans built especially for you

- Get a free eBook or video every month

- Mapt is fully searchable

- Copy and paste, print, and bookmark content

## Packt.com

Did you know that Packt offers eBook versions of every book published, with PDF and ePub files available? You can upgrade to the eBook version at www.packt.com and as a print book customer, you are entitled to a discount on the eBook copy. Get in touch with us at customercare@packtpub.com for more details.

At www.packt.com, you can also read a collection of free technical articles, sign up for a range of free newsletters, and receive exclusive discounts and offers on Packt books and eBooks.

# Contributors

## About the Author

**Kaelen Medeiros** is a content quality developer at DataCamp, where she works to improve course content and tracks quality metrics across the company. She also works as a data scientist/developer for HealthLabs, who develop automated methods for analyzing large amounts of medical data. She received her MS in biostatistics from Louisiana State University Health Sciences Center in 2016. Outside of work, she has one cat, listens to way too many podcasts, and enjoys running.

## Packt is Searching for Authors Like You

If you're interested in becoming an author for Packt, please visit authors.packtpub.com and apply today. We have worked with thousands of developers and tech professionals, just like you, to help them share their insight with the global tech community. You can make a general application, apply for a specific hot topic that we are recruiting an author for, or submit your own idea.

# Table of Contents

# Preface

Demand for data scientists is growing exponentially and demand in the US is expected to increase by 28 percent by the year 2020, with this trend reflected across the world. R is a tool often used by data scientists to clean, examine, analyze, and report on data. It is a great starting point for those familiar with analysis in Excel or MS SQL and is an excellent place to begin to learn programming fundamentals.

This book begins by addressing the setup of R and RStudio on the machine and progresses from there, demonstrating how to import datasets, clean them, and explore their contents. It balances theory and exercises, and contains multiple open-ended activities that use real-life business scenarios for you to practice and apply your newly acquired skills in a highly relevant context. We have included over 50 practical activities and exercises across 11 topics, along with a mini project that will allow you to begin your data science project portfolio. With this book, we have created a definitive guide to beginning data science in R.

## Who This Book is for

This book is for analysts who are looking to grow their data science skills beyond the tools they have used before, such as MS Excel and other statistical tools.

## What This Book Covers

Chapter 1, *Introduction to R*, deals with installation of R, RStudio, and other useful packages, and talks about variable types and data structures. The chapter then introduces the different kinds of loops that can be used in R, explains how to import and export data, and also talks about getting help with R programming.

Chapter 2, *Data Visualization and Graphics*, covers the basic plots built into R and how to create them, and then introduces ggplot, a popular graphics package in R. Finally, the chapter briefly talks about two tools, Shiny and Plotly, that can be used to design interactive plots.

Chapter 3, *Data Management*, discusses how to create and manipulate factor variables, examine data using tables, apply the family of functions to generate summaries, and split, combine, merge, or join datasets in R.

The *Appendix* contains the solutions to all the activities within the chapters.

# To Get the Most Out of This Book

You will require a computer system with at least an i3 processor, 2 GB RAM, 10 GB of storage space, and an internet connection. Along with this, you would require the following software:

1. Operating System: Windows 8 64-bit
2. R and Rstudio
3. Browsers (Google Chrome and Mozilla Firefox - latest versions)

# Download the Example Code Files

You can download the example code files for this book from your account at www.packt.com. If you purchased this book elsewhere, you can visit www.packt.com/support and register to have the files emailed directly to you.

You can download the code files by following these steps:

1. Log in or register at www.packt.com.
2. Select the **SUPPORT** tab.
3. Click on **Code Downloads & Errata**.
4. Enter the name of the book in the **Search** box and follow the onscreen instructions.

Once the file is downloaded, please make sure that you unzip or extract the folder using the latest version of:

- WinRAR/7-Zip for Windows
- Zipeg/iZip/UnRarX for Mac
- 7-Zip/PeaZip for Linux

The code bundle for the book is also hosted on GitHub at https://github.com/TrainingByPackt/R-Programming-Fundamentals. In case there's an update to the code, it will be updated on the existing GitHub repository.

We also have other code bundles from our rich catalog of books and videos available at https://github.com/PacktPublishing/. Check them out!

# Conventions Used

There are a number of text conventions used throughout this book.

`CodeInText`: Indicates code words in text, database table names, folder names, filenames, file extensions, pathnames, dummy URLs, user input, and Twitter handles. Here is an example: "Mount the downloaded `WebStorm-10*.dmg` disk image file as another disk in your system."

A block of code is set as follows:

```
html, body, #map {
 height: 100%;
 margin: 0;
 padding: 0
}
```

When we wish to draw your attention to a particular part of a code block, the relevant lines or items are set in bold:

```
[default]
exten => s,1,Dial(Zap/1|30)
exten => s,2,Voicemail(u100)
exten => s,102,Voicemail(b100)
exten => i,1,Voicemail(s0)
```

Any command-line input or output is written as follows:

```
$ mkdir css
$ cd css
```

**Bold**: Indicates a new term, an important word, or words that you see onscreen. For example, words in menus or dialog boxes appear in the text like this. Here is an example: "Select **System info** from the **Administration** panel."

Warnings or important notes appear like this.

Tips and tricks appear like this.

# Get in Touch

Feedback from our readers is always welcome.

**General feedback**: If you have questions about any aspect of this book, mention the book title in the subject of your message and email us at customercare@packtpub.com.

**Errata**: Although we have taken every care to ensure the accuracy of our content, mistakes do happen. If you have found a mistake in this book, we would be grateful if you would report this to us. Please visit www.packt.com/submit-errata, selecting your book, clicking on the Errata Submission Form link, and entering the details.

**Piracy**: If you come across any illegal copies of our works in any form on the Internet, we would be grateful if you would provide us with the location address or website name. Please contact us at copyright@packt.com with a link to the material.

**If you are interested in becoming an author**: If there is a topic that you have expertise in and you are interested in either writing or contributing to a book, please visit authors.packtpub.com.

# Reviews

Please leave a review. Once you have read and used this book, why not leave a review on the site that you purchased it from? Potential readers can then see and use your unbiased opinion to make purchase decisions, we at Packt can understand what you think about our products, and our authors can see your feedback on their book. Thank you!

For more information about Packt, please visit packt.com.

 All the solutions to the activities are present in the *Appendix* section.

# Introduction to R

One tool that statisticians—and now data scientists as well—often use for data cleaning, analysis, and reporting is the R programming language.

In this chapter, we'll begin by looking at the basics of using R as a programming language and as a statistical analysis tool, and we'll also install a few useful R packages that we will continue to use throughout the book.

By the end of this chapter, you will be able to:

- Install R packages for use throughout the book
- Use R as a calculator for basic arithmetic
- Utilize different data structures
- Control program flow by writing if-else, for, and while loops
- Import and export data to and from CSV, Excel, and SQL

## Using R and RStudio, and Installing Useful Packages

R is a programming language intended for use for statistical analysis. Additionally, it can be utilized in an object-oriented or functional way. Specifically, it is an implementation of S, an interactive statistical programming language. R was initially released in August 1993. It is maintained today by the R Development Core Team.

RStudio is an incredibly useful **Integrated Development Environment** (**IDE**) for writing and using R. Many data scientists use RStudio for writing R, as it provides a console window, a code editor, tools to help create plots and graphics, and can even be integrated with GitHub to support version control.

While R does share some functionality with Microsoft Excel, it allows you to have more control over your data, and you can add on a variety of packages that allow statistical functionality out of the box—you won't have to build a formula to conduct a survival analysis; you can just install the survival package and use that!

 Ensure that you have R and RStudio installed on your system. RStudio will not work if you don't have R installed on your machine; they must be installed separately. Once they are both installed, you can open RStudio and use that without having an R window open.

# Using R and RStudio

Out of the box, R is completely usable. Open R on your machine. Let's use R for some basic arithmetic such as addition, multiplication, subtraction, and division. The following screenshot demonstrates this:

```
> 10 + 2
[1] 12
> 5 * 5
[1] 25
> 98 - 14
[1] 84
> 8 / 2
[1] 4
>
```

It also provides functions such as sum() and sqrt() for addition and calculation of the square root. The following screenshot shows this in action:

```
> sqrt(25)
[1] 5
> sum(5, 6, 7, 8, 9)
[1] 35
>
```

R can—and will—do basic arithmetic like a calculator, using symbols you're familiar with. One you may not have used before is exponentiate, where you use two asterisks, for example, 4 ** 2, which you can read as 4 to the power of 2.

Once you want to start doing math beyond basic arithmetic, such as finding square roots or summing many numbers, you have to start using functions.

## Executing Basic Functions in the R Console

Let's now try and execute the sum() and sqrt() functions in R. Follow the steps given below:

1. Open the R console on your system.
2. Type the code as follows:

```
sum(1, 2, 3, 4, 5)
sqrt(144)
```

3. Execute the code.

**Output**: The preceding code provides the following output:

```
[1]    15
[1]    12
```

Functions such as sum() and sqrt() are called **base functions**, which are built into R. This means that they come pre-installed when R is downloaded.

We could build all of our code right in the R console, but eventually, we might want to see our files, a list of everything in our global environment, and more, so instead, we'll use RStudio. Close R, and when it asks you to save the workspace image, for now, click **Don't Save**. (More explanation on workspace images and saving will come later in this chapter.)

Open RStudio. We'll use RStudio for all of our code development from here on. One major benefit of RStudio is that we can use **Projects**, which will organize all of the files for analysis in one folder on our computer automatically. Projects will keep all of the parts of your analysis organized in one space in a chosen folder on your machine. Any time you start a new project, you should start a new project in RStudio by going to **File | New Project**, as shown in the below screenshot, or by clicking the new project button (blue, with a green plus sign 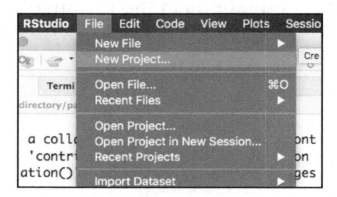 ).

Creating a project from a **New Directory** allows us to create a folder on our drive (here E:\) to store all code files, data, and anything else associated with the book. If there was an existing folder on our drive that we'd like to make the directory for the project, we would choose the **Existing Directory** option. The **Version Control** option allows you to clone a repository from GitHub or another version control site. It makes a copy of the project stored on GitHub and saves it on your computer:

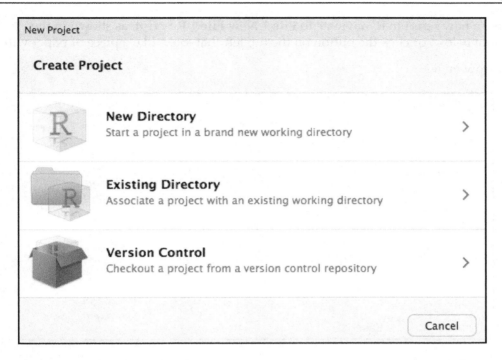

The working directory in R is the folder where all of the code files and output will be saved. It should be the same as the folder you choose when you create a project from a new or existing directory. To verify the working directory at any time, use the getwd() function. It will print the working directory as a character string (you can tell because it has quotation marks around it). The working directory can be changed at any time by using the following syntax:

```
setwd("new location/on the/computer")
```

To create a new script in R, navigate to **File** | **New File** | **R Script**, as shown in the screenshot below, or click the button on the top left that looks like a piece of paper with a green arrow on it 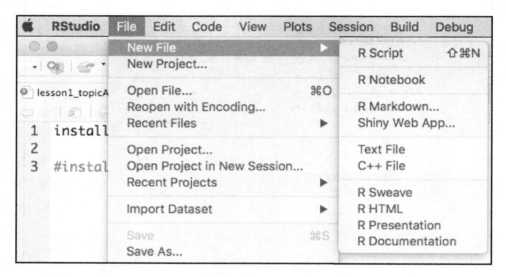 .

Inside **New File**, there are options to create quite a few different things that you might use in R. We'll be creating R scripts throughout this book.

Custom functions are fairly straightforward to create in R. Generally, they should be created using the following syntax:

```
name_of_function <- function(input1, input2){
operation to be performed with the inputs
}
```

The example custom function is as follows:

```
area_triangle <- function(base, height){
0.5 * base * height
}
```

Once the custom function code has been run, it will display in the **Global Environment** in the upper right corner and is now available for use in your RStudio project, as shown in the following screenshot:

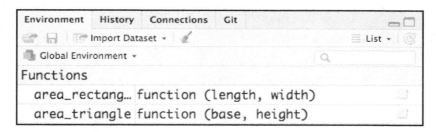

One crucial step upon exiting RStudio or when you close your computer is to save a copy of the global environment. This will save any data or custom functions in the environment for later use and is done with the `save.image()` function, into which you'll need to enter a character string of what you want the saved file to be called, for example, `introDSwR.RData`. It will always be named with the extension `.RData`. If you were to open your project again some other time and want to load the saved environment, you use the `load()` function, with the same character string inside it.

# Setting up a New Project

Let us now set up a new project that we will use throughout the book. We will create an R project, script, custom function, and save an image of the global environment. Follow the steps given below:

1. Open RStudio.
2. Navigate to **File | New Project** to start a new project:
    - Start with a new directory and save it in a place on your computer that makes sense to you.
    - Save the project with the name `IntroToDSwRCourse`.
3. Check the working directory using the `getwd()` function and be sure it's the same folder you chose to save your project in.
4. Start a new script. Save the script with the filename `lesson1_exercise.R`.
5. Write a custom function, `area_rectangle()`, which calculates the area of a rectangle, with the following code:

```
area_rectangle <- function(length, width){
length * width
}
```

6. Try out `area_rectangle()` with the following sets of lengths and widths:
   - 5, 10
   - 80, 7
   - 48209302930, 4

The code will be as follows:

```
area_rectangle(5, 10)
area_rectangle(80, 70)
area_rectangle(48209302930, 4)
```

7. Save an image of the global environment for later; name the file `introToDSwR.RData`.

**Output**: The output you get after executing the `getwd()` function will be the folder on your computer that you have chosen to save your project in.

The area of the rectangle with different lengths will be provided as follows:

```
[1] 50
[1] 5600
[1] 192837211720
```

R and RStudio will be our main tools throughout this book for statistical analysis and programming. We've now seen how to create a new project, a new R script, and how to save a workspace image for use later.

# Installing Packages

In this chapter, we've already seen some of the base functions that are built into R. We also built a few custom functions, `area_triangle()` and `area_rectangle()`, in the last section.

Now, let's talk about packages. Anyone can write an R package of useful functions and publish it for use by others. Packages are usually made available on the **Comprehensive R Archive Network (CRAN)** website, or **Bioconductor**, a collection of packages for bioinformatics and other uses. Both these sites conduct a thorough review of submitted packages before publishing them on their sites, so package developers often keep beta versions of packages, or those that are useful but may not pass the inspections, on GitHub.

RStudio makes installing packages very easy. There are two ways to do so: either type `install.packages("package_name")` in a script or your console, or you can navigate to the **Packages** tab in the lower right window and click **Install**, which will show a window that allows you to type the names of the packages that are available on CRAN. You can even install multiple packages if you separate them with a comma. You'll want to keep **Install dependencies** checked, as this will install any packages that the package you've chosen depends on to run successfully—you'll want those! Let's see this in the following screenshot:

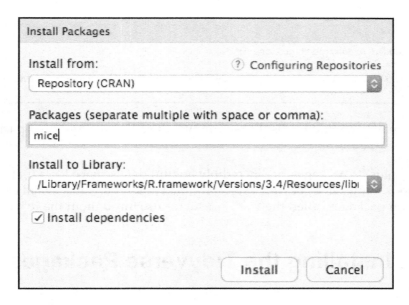

Let's now use two different methods to install R packages. Follow these steps:

- Install the `survival` package using the following code:

```
install.packages("survival")
```

- Install the `mice` package using the **Install** button on the **Packages** tab.

**Output**: The following should be displayed on your console:

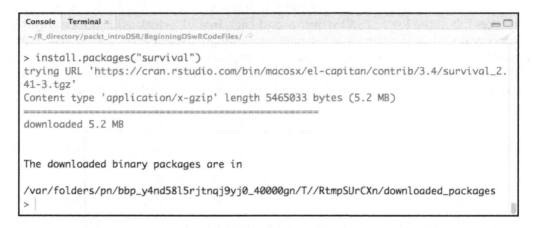

The same information should be displayed once you install `mice`, with that package's name subbed in for `survival`.

R and RStudio, plus its packages, are incredibly helpful data science tools that will be the focus of this book. Now, let's get your project for the book set up, and install a set of incredibly useful packages called the `Tidyverse`, for use throughout the rest of this book.

# Activity: Installing the Tidyverse Packages

**Scenario**

You have been assigned the task of developing a report using R. You need to install the `Tidyverse` packages to develop that report.

**Aim**

To install `Tidyverse`, a set of useful packages that will be used later in the book. Load the inbuilt datasets into the project.

**Prerequisites**

Make sure that you have R and RStudio installed on your machine.

**Steps for completion**

1. Install the `Tidyverse` package using the `install.package()` function.

2. Load the `ggplot2` library and the built-in `msleep` dataset.

 Note that `msleep` is a built-in dataset in the ggplot2 package. We'll use R built-in datasets throughout this book.

3. Save the global image of the environment for use later use.

This activity was crucial. We've added a dataset and the `Tidyverse` packages to the project we intend to use for the rest of the book. We've also saved a copy of our global environment to our working directory. The `Tidyverse` packages, `dplyr`, `ggplot2`, `tidyr`, and a few others, will be very helpful throughout this book and in your data science work.

# Variable Types and Data Structures

In this section, we'll begin first with an exploration of different variable types: numeric, character, and dates. We'll then look at different data structures in R: vectors, lists, matrices, and data frames.

# Variable Types

Variable types exist in all programming languages and will tell the computer how to store and access a variable.

First, know that all variables created in R will have a class and a type. You can look at the class or type of anything in R using the `class()` and `typeof()` functions, respectively.

The class of an object is a broad designation, for example, `character`, `numeric`, `integer`, and `date`. These are very broad categories, and type elaborates more specifically on what type of variable it is, for example, a variable of class `date` can be of type `character` or `POSIXct`, depending on how it is stored. Type drills down into the details of a variable and how it's been stored in R, though sometimes class and type can be the same. For example, integers are of class and type `integer`, and character strings are of type and class `character`. Let's examine the following code snippet:

```
x <- 4.2
class(x)
typeof(x)
```

The preceding code provides the following output:

```
[1] "numeric"
[1] "double"
```

In this snippet, x has a class `numeric`, because it is a number, but also has a type `double` because it is a decimal number. This is because all numeric data in R is of type `double` unless the object has been explicitly declared to be an `integer`. Let's look at some examples of different classes and types.

## Numeric and Integers

The `numeric` data class includes all numbers except integers, which are their own separate class in R. Anything of class `numeric` will be of type `double`, unless it is explicitly declared as an `integer`. To create an `integer`, you must type a capital letter, L, after a whole number.

Let's now create and check the `class()` and `typeof()` of different numeric objects in R. Follow the steps given below:

1. Create the following numeric objects:

   ```
   x <- 12.7
   y <- 8L
   z <- 950
   ```

2. Check the class and type of each using `class()` and `typeof()`, respectively, as follows:

   ```
   class(x)
   typeof(x)

   class(y)
   typeof(y)

   class(z)
   typeof(z)
   ```

**Output**: The preceding code provides the following output:

```
[1] "numeric"
[1] "double"
[1] "integer"
[1] "integer"
[1] "numeric"
[1] "double"
```

# Character

Character data is always mentioned in quotation marks; anything contained in quotation marks is called a character string. Usually, character data is of both class and type character.

Let's create and check the class() and typeof() of different character objects in R. Follow the steps given below:

1. Create the following objects:

```
a <- "apple"
b <- "7"
c <- "9-5-2016"
```

2. Check the class and type of each using class() and typeof(), respectively, as follows:

```
class(a)
typeof(a)

class(b)
typeof(b)

class(c)
typeof(c)
```

**Output**: The preceding code provides the following output:

```
[1] "character"
[1] "character"
[1] "character"
[1] "character"
[1] "character"
[1] "character"
```

# Dates

Dates are a special type of data in R, and are distinct from the date types `POSIXct` and `POSIXlt`, which represent calendar dates and times in more formal ways.

Let's create and check the `class()` and `typeof()` of different date objects in R. Follow these steps:

1. Create the objects using the following code:

```
e <- as.Date("2016-09-05")
f <- as.POSIXct("2018-04-05")
```

2. Check the class and type of each by using `class()` and `typeof()`, respectively, as follows:

```
class(e)
typeof(e)

class(f)
typeof(f)
```

**Output**: The preceding code provides the following output:

```
[1] "Date"
[1] "double"
[1] "POSIXct" "POSIXt"
[1] "double"
```

One nice thing about R is that we can change objects from one type to another using the `as.*()` function family. If we have a variable, `var`, which currently has the value of 5, but as a character string, we can cast it to numeric data type using `as.numeric()` and to an integer using `as.integer()`, which the following code demonstrates:

```
#char to numeric, integer
var <- "5"

var_num <- as.numeric(var)
class(var_num)
typeof(var_num)

var_int <- as.integer(var)
class(var_int)
typeof(var_int).
```

Conversely, we can go the other way and cast the var_num and var_int variables back to the character data type using as.character(). The following code demonstrates this:

```
#numeric, integer to char
var <- 5

#numeric to char
var_char <- as.character(var_num)
class(var_char)
typeof(var_char)

#int to char
var_char2 <- as.character(var_int)
class(var_char2)
typeof(var_char2)
```

A character string can be converted into a Date, but it does need to be in the format Year-Month-Day (Y-M-D) so that you can use the as.Date() function, as shown in the following code:

```
#char to date
date <- "18-03-29"
Date <- as.Date(date)
class(Date)
typeof(Date)
```

There are formatting requirements for dates for them to save correctly. For example, the following code will not work:

```
date2 <- as.Date("03-29-18")
```

It will throw the following error:

```
Error in charToDate(x) : character string is not in a standard unambiguous
format
```

It will be important to understand variable types throughout a data science project. It would be very difficult to both clean and summarize data if you're unsure of its type. In Chapter 3, *Data Management*, we'll also introduce another variable type: factors.

# Activity: Identifying Variable Classes and Types

## Scenario

You need to write some code for classifying the data correctly for easy report generation. The following is the provided data:

| Variable | Class | Type |
|---|---|---|
| "John Smith" | | |
| 16 | | |
| 10L | | |
| 3.92 | | |
| -10 | | |
| "03-28-02" | | |
| as.Date("02-03-28") | | |

## Aim

To identify different classes and types of data in R.

## Prerequisites

A pencil or pen, plus RStudio and R installed on your machine.

## Steps for completion

1. Fill in the table provided with the class and type of each variable.
2. Use the `class()` or `typeof()` functions if you get stuck, but first try and fill it in without the code!

# Data Structures

There are a few different data structures in R that are crucial to understand, as they directly pertain to the use of data! These include vectors, matrices, and dataframes. We'll discuss how to tell the difference between all of these, along with how to create and manipulate them.

Data structures are extremely important in R for manipulating, exploring, and analyzing data. There are a few key structures that will hold the different types of variables we discussed in the last subsection, and more. R uses different words for some of these data structures than other programming languages, but the idea behind them is the same.

# Vectors

A vector is an object that holds a collection of various data elements in R, though they are limited because everything inside of a vector must all belong to the same variable type. You can create a vector using the method `c()`, for example:

```
vector_example <- c(1, 2, 3, 4)
```

In the above snippet, the method `c()` creates a vector named `vector_example`. It will have a length of four and be of class `numeric`. You use `c()` to create any type of vector by inputting a comma-separated list of the items you'd like inside the vector. If you input different classes of objects inside the vector (such as numeric and character strings), it will default to one of them.

In the following code, we can see an example where the class of the vector is a `character` because of the `B` in position 2:

```
vector_example_2 <- c(1, "B", 3)
class(vector_example_2)
```

**Output**: The preceding code provides the following output:

```
[1] "character"
```

To access a certain item in the vector, you can use indexing. R is a 1-indexed language, meaning all counting starts at 1 (versus other languages, such as Python, which are 0-indexed—that is, in Python, the first element of the array is said to be at the 0th position).

The first item in a vector can be accessed using `vector[1]`, and so on. If the index doesn't exist in the vector, R will simply output an `NA`, which is R's default way of indicating a missing value. We'll cover missing values in R at length in `Chapter 3`, *Data Management*.

Let us now use `c()` to create a vector, examine its class and type, and access different elements of the vector using vector indexing. Follow the steps given below:

1. Create the vectors `twenty` and `alphabet` using the following code:

```
twenty <- c(1:20)
alphabet <- c(letters)
```

2. Check the class and type of twenty and alphabet using `class()` and `typeof()`, respectively, as follows:

```
class(twenty)
typeof(twenty)

class(alphabet)
typeof(alphabet)
```

3. Find the numbers at the following positions in `twenty` using vector indexing:

```
twenty[5]
twenty[17]
twenty[25]
```

4. Find the letters at the following positions in the alphabet using vector indexing:

```
alphabet[6]
alphabet[23]
alphabet[33]
```

**Output**: The code we write will be as follows:

```
twenty <- c(1:20)
alphabet <- c(letters)
class(twenty)
typeof(twenty)
class(alphabet)
typeof(alphabet)
twenty[5]
twenty[17]
twenty[25]
alphabet[6]
alphabet[23]
alphabet[33]
```

The output we get after executing it is as follows:

```
[1] "integer"
[1] "integer"
[1] "character"
[1] "character"
[1] 5
[1] 17
[1] NA
[1] "f"
[1] "w"
[1] NA
```

# Lists

A list is different from a vector because it can hold many different types of R objects inside it, including other lists. If you have experience programming in another language, you may be familiar with lists, but if not, don't worry! You can create a list in R using the `list()` function, as shown in the following example:

```
L1 <- list(1, "2", "Hello", "cat", 12, list(1, 2, 3))
```

Let's walk through the elements of this list. First, we have the number 1. Then, a character string, "2", followed by the character string "Hello", the character string "cat", the number 12, and then a nested list, which contains the numbers 1, 2, and 3.

Accessing these different parts of the list that we just created is slightly different—now, you are using list indexing, which means using double square brackets to look at the different items.

You'll need to enter `L1[[1]]` to view the number 1 and `L1[[4]]` to see "cat".

To get inside the nested list, you'll have to use `L1[[6]][1]` to see the number 1. `L1[[6]]` gets us to the nested list, located at position 6, and `L1[[6]][1]` allows us to access the first element of the nested list, in this case, number 1. The following screenshot shows the output of this code:

```
> L1 <- list(1, "2", "Hello", "cat", 12, list(1, 2, 3))
>
> L1[[1]]
[1] 1
> L1[[4]]
[1] "cat"
> L1[[6]][1]
[[1]]
[1] 1
```

Lists can also be changed into other data structures. We could turn a list into a dataframe, but this particular list, because it contains a nested list, will not coerce to a vector. The following code demonstrates this:

```
L1_df <- as.data.frame(L1)
class(L1_df)
L1_vec <- as.vector(L1)
class(L1_vec)
```

The following screenshot shows the output of this code:

```
> L1_df <- as.data.frame(L1)
> class(L1_df)
[1] "data.frame"
> L1_vec <- as.vector(L1)
> class(L1_vec)
[1] "list"
```

# Matrices

A matrix is a 2D vector with rows and columns. In R, one requirement for matrices is that every data element stored inside it be of the same type (all character, all numeric, and so on). This allows you to perform arithmetic operations with matrices, if, for example, you have two that are both numeric.

Let's use matrix() to create a matrix, examine its class, use rownames() and colnames() to set row and column names, and access different elements of the matrix using multiple methods. Follow the steps given below:

1. Use matrix() to create matrix1, a 3 x 3 matrix containing the numbers 1:12 by column, using the following code:

   ```
   matrix1 <- matrix(c(1:12), nrow = 3, ncol = 3, byrow = FALSE)
   ```

2. Create matrix2 similarly, also 3 x 3, and fill it with 1:12 by row, using the following code:

   ```
   matrix2 <- matrix(c(1:12), nrow = 3, ncol = 3, byrow = TRUE)
   ```

3. Set the row and column names of matrix1 with the following:

   ```
   rownames(matrix1) <- c("one", "two", "three")
   colnames(matrix1) <- c("one", "two", "three")
   ```

4. Find the elements at the following positions in `matrix1` using matrix indexing:

```
matrix1[1, 2]
matrix1["one",]
matrix1[,"one"]
matrix1["one","one"]
```

The output of the code is as follows:

```
> #matrix indexing
> matrix1[1, 2]
[1] 4
> matrix1["one",]
  one   two three
    1     4     7
```

# Dataframes

A dataframe in R is a 2D object where the columns can contain data of different classes and types. This is very useful for practical data storage.

Dataframes can be created by using `as.data.frame()` on applicable objects or by column- or row-binding vectors using `cbind.data.frame()` or `rbind.data.frame()`. Here's an example where we can create a list of nested lists and turn it into a data frame:

```
list_for_df <- list(list(1:3), list(4:6), list(7:9))
example_df <- as.data.frame(list_for_df)
```

`example_df` will have three rows and three columns. We can set the column names just as we did with the matrix, though it isn't common practice in R to set the row names for most analyses. It can be demonstrated by the following code:

```
colnames(example_df) <- c("one", "two", "three")
```

We have covered a few of the key data structures in R in this section, and we have seen how to create and manipulate them. Let's try a few examples.

# Activity: Creating Vectors, Lists, Matrices, and Dataframes

**Scenario**

You have been asked to create vectors, lists, matrices, and dataframes that store information about yourself. The expected output is as follows:

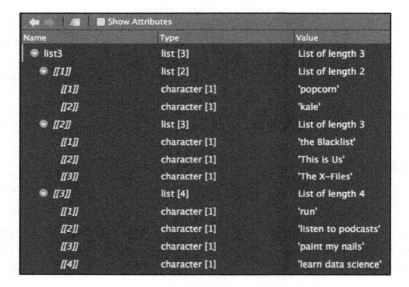

**Aim**

To create vectors, lists, matrices, and dataframes.

**Prerequisites**

Make sure that you have R and RStudio installed on your machine.

**Steps for Completion**

1. Open a new R script and save it as a file called `lesson1_activityB2.R`.

2. Create vectors for the following:

    - The numbers 1:10

    - The letters A:Z, with the first four numbers and letters alternating

Hint: type ?LETTERS into your console.

3. Create lists for the following:
   - The numbers 1:10
   - The letters A:Z
   - A list of lists:
     - Your favorite foods (two or more)
     - Your favorite TV shows (three or more)
     - Things you like to do (four or more)

4. Create matrices of numbers and letters by using the following steps:
   1. First, try using cbind() to combine the vector 1:10 and the vector A:Z. What happens?
   2. Figure out a way to combine these two into a matrix, albeit one that will be coerced to character type (despite the numeric column).

5. Create dataframes using the following steps:
   1. Coerce your matrix solution from the previous second bullet point into a dataframe. View it and take note of the type of each variable.
   2. Use rbind.data.frame() to build a data frame where the rows increase by five until 25, for example, 5, 10, 15, 20, 25.
   3. View it and notice how ugly the column names are. Give it better names ("one" through "five") with the names() function.

# Basic Flow Control

Flow Control includes different kinds of loops that you can use in R, such as the if/else, for, and while loops. While many of the concepts are very similar to how flow control and loops are used in other programming languages, they may be written differently in R.

 Generally speaking, most loops are not considered best practice for coding in R. Some alternatives to loops, especially for loops, include the apply family of functions and functions contained in the purrr package, which you are encouraged to look up and learn about after this book.

# If/else

The `if` loop will only run a block of code if a certain condition is TRUE. It can be paired with `else` statements to create an `if/else` loop. This will work similarly to an `if/else` loop in other programming languages, though the syntax may be different.

The usual syntax for using `if` is as follows:

```
if(test_condition){
some_action
}
```

Here, the action only occurs if the `test_condition` evaluates to TRUE, so, for example, if you wrote 4 < 5, the code in the curly braces would definitely run.

If there's something you want to happen, even if the test condition isn't true, you would use an `if/else`, where the syntax usually looks like this:

```
if(test_expression){
some_action
}else{
some_other_action
}
```

Even if the `test_expression` isn't true, `some_other_action` will still happen. Finally, you can evaluate multiple test conditions with `if/else if/else`, as shown in the following syntax:

```
if(test_expression){
some_action
}else if(another_test_expression){
some_other_action
}else{
yet_another_action
}
```

Let's do some actual examples to help illustrate these points. Take a look at the following code:

```
var <- "Hello"
if(class(var) == "character"){
print("Your variable is a character string.")
}
```

What output would you expect here? What output would you expect if the variable was assigned the value `var <- 5` instead? When `var` is "Hello", the `if` statement is TRUE, and "Your variable is a character string" will print to the console. However, when `var` is 5, nothing happens, because we didn't specify an `else` statement.

With the following code, when `var` is 5, something will print:

```
var <- 5
if(class(var) == "character"){
print("Your variable is a character string.")
}else{
print("Your variable is not a character")
}
```

Because we specified `else`, we will see the output "Your variable is not a character." This isn't very informative, however, so let's expand and use an `else if`:

```
if(class(var) == "character"){
print("Your variable is a character string.")
}else if (class(var) == "numeric"){
print("Your variable is numeric")
}else{
print("Your variable is something besides character or numeric.")
}
```

If `var` is 5, now we'll see "Your variable is numeric". What if `var` was a date? What would print then? Yup, you got it! "Your variable is something besides character or numeric" will print to the console.

# For loop

`For` loops are often used to go through every column or row of a dataframe in R.

Say, for example, that we're interested in the mean of all of the numeric columns of the built-in `iris` dataset (which is four out of the five—everything but the `Species` column, which is a factor variable of character strings indicating the species of each iris.) We could type, four times, `mean(iris$Sepal.Length)`, with each input variable name changing each time. However, a far more efficient way to complete this exercise would be to use a `for` loop.

If we simply want to print the means to the console, we could use a `for` loop as follows:

```
for(i in seq_along(iris)){
print(mean(iris[[i]]))
}
```

The output will be as follows:

```
> for(i in seq_along(iris)){
+      print(mean(iris[[i]]))
+ }
[1] 5.843333
[1] 3.057333
[1] 3.758
[1] 1.199333
[1] NA
Warning message:
In mean.default(iris[[i]]) :
   argument is not numeric or logical: returning NA
```

We'll come back to the output, especially that warning message, in a second—first, let's break down the components of the for loop. The syntax will always be as follows:

```
for(i in a range of numbers){
some_action
}
```

In this particular `for` loop, we chose `i` as our iterator variable. A `for` loop in R will automatically iterate this variable, which means that every time it reaches the end of the loop, it will increase `i` by one. You might have noticed that once the loop has finished completing, `i` was added to the global environment as a **Value**, 5L (which means it's an integer, the number 5). Our iterator will always get added to the environment when a loop concludes.

It is displayed on the screen, as shown in the following screenshot:

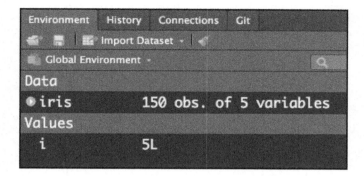

The R function `seq_along()` is very helpful for the `for` loops, because it automatically moves along the number of columns of the dataframe (if that's the input) or more generally, iterates along the number of items contained in whatever is input into it.

We also chose to print the mean of each column in this particular `for` loop. Accessing the columns is done using indexing, so when `i = 1`, `iris[[i]]` is equal to the `Sepal.Length` variable, which is column 1, and so on. We got an error for column 5, because it isn't numeric (the `Species` variable!) Species doesn't have a mean, because it's a character variable.

This is actually a great example of where we can combine for loops with an `if` statement. Take a look at the following code:

```
for(i in seq_along(iris)){
    if(class(iris[[i]]) == "numeric"){
        print(mean(iris[[i]]))
    }
}
```

The `if` statement here will only print the mean of an `iris` column if the class of that column is numeric (which makes sense, since only numeric columns should have means!) The output is now only as follows:

```
[1] 5.843333
[1] 3.057333
[1] 3.758
[1] 1.199333
```

If we're really feeling fancy, we could have even added an `else` statement with a different message for when the class of a column isn't numeric, such as in this loop:

```
for(i in seq_along(iris)){
    if(class(iris[[i]]) == "numeric"){
        print(mean(iris[[i]]))
    }else{
        print(paste("Variable", i, "isn't numeric"))
    }
}
```

The output is as follows:

```
[1] 5.843333
[1] 3.057333
[1] 3.758
[1] 1.199333
[1] "Variable 5 isn't numeric"
```

`seq_along()` returns a sequence of numbers and makes `for` loops more straightforward. However, if you need to iterate using any other function, the syntax of the `for` statement will change slightly. The following code will print every row of the `Species` column in `iris`:

```
for(i in 1:nrow(iris)){
    print(iris[i, "Sepal.Width"])
}
```

You have to explicitly use `1:nrow(iris)` in the `for` statement, or this loop will not run. `nrow()` simply returns the number of rows of `iris` versus the entire sequence of the number of columns that `seq_along()` returns as shown below:

```
nrow(iris)
[1] 150
seq_along(iris)
[1] 1 2 3 4 5
```

# While loop

Versus the `for` loop, which walks through an iterator (usually, this is a sequence of numbers), a `while` loop will not iterate through a sequence of numbers for you. Instead, it requires you to add a line of code inside the body of the loop that increments or decrements your iterator, usually `i`. Generally, the syntax for a while loop is as follows:

```
while(test_expression){
some_action
}
```

Here, the action will only occur if the `test_expression` is TRUE. Otherwise, R will not enter the curly braces and run what's inside them. If a test expression is never TRUE, it's possible that a `while` loop may never run!

A classic example of a `while` loop is one that prints out numbers, such as the following:

```
i = 0
while(i <= 5){
    print(paste("loop", i))
    i = i + 1
}
```

The output of the preceding code is as follows:

```
[1] "loop 0"
[1] "loop 1"
[1] "loop 2"
[1] "loop 3"
[1] "loop 4"
[1] "loop 5"
```

Because we set our test expression to be `i` less than or equal to 5, the loop stopped printing once `i` was 6, and R broke out of the `while` loop. This is good, because infinite loops (loops that never stop running) are definitely possible. If the `while` loop test expression is never FALSE, the loop will never stop, as shown in the following code:

```
while(TRUE){
print("yes!")
}
```

The output will be as follows:

```
[1] "yes!"
[1] "yes!"
[1] "yes!"
[1] "yes!"
......
```

This is an example of an infinite loop. If you're concerned about them, R does have a break statement, which will jump out of the `while` loop, but you'll see the following error:

```
Error: no loop for break/next, jumping to top level
```

This is because break statements in R are meant more for breaking out of nested loops, where there is one inside another.

It's also possible (though you likely wouldn't code this on purpose, as it will be an error of some kind) for a `while` loop to never run. For example, if we forgot that i is in our global environment, and that it equals 5, the following loop will never run:

```
while(i < 5){
    print(paste(i, "is this number"))
    i = i + 1
}
```

Let's now try and get a feel of how loops work in R. We will try to predict what the loop code will print. Follow the steps below:

1. Examine the following code snippet. Try to predict what the output will be:

```
vec <- seq(1:10)
for(num in seq_along(vec)){
    if(num %% 2 == 0){
        print(paste(num, "is even"))
    } else{
        print(paste(num, "is odd"))
    }
}
```

2. Examine the following code snippet. Try to predict what the output will be:

```
example <- data.frame(color = c("red", "blue", "green"), number =
c(1, 2, 3))
for(i in seq(nrow(example))){
print(example[i,1])
}
```

3. Examine the following code snippet. Try to predict what the output will be:

```
var <- 5
while(var > 0){
    print(var)
    var = var - 1
}
```

**Output**: The output for the first step will be as follows:

```
[1] "1 is odd"
[1] "2 is even"
[1] "3 is odd"
[1] "4 is even"
[1] "5 is odd"
[1] "6 is even"
[1] "7 is odd"
[1] "8 is even"
[1] "9 is odd"
[1] "10 is even"
```

The output for the second step will be as follows:

```
[1] red
Levels: blue green red
[1] blue
Levels: blue green red
[1] green
Levels: blue green red
```

The output for the third step will be as follows:

```
[1] 5
[1] 4
[1] 3
[1] 2
[1] 1
```

It's important as you code in R that you understand how loops work, both because other people will write code with them and so you need to understand how other methods that can be substituted in for loops in R work.

# Activity: Building Basic Loops

**Scenario**

You've been asked to create loops to examine the variables inside the `ChickWeight` and `iris` built-in R datasets.

**Aim**

To implement of `if`, `if/else`, `for`, and `while` loops, including combinations of the four types of loops.

**Prerequisites**

You must have R and RStudio installed on your machine.

**Steps for Completion**

1. Open a new R script and save it with the name `lesson1_activityC.R`.
2. Load the `iris` and `ChickWeight` built-in R datasets. You will need to load them in separate `data()` functions.
3. `If` loop: Set `var = 100` and create an `if` statement that prints **Big number** if `var` divided by five is greater than or equal to 25.
4. `If/else`: Expand and add an `else` statement that prints **Not as big of a number**
5. `If/else if/else`: In the middle, add an `else if` statement that prints **Medium number** if `var` divided by five is greater than or equal to 20.
6. `For`: Create a `for` loop that prints out **Iris NUMBER is SPECIES** for each row of iris:

 Remember that `seq_along()` is for moving along columns. To move down rows, use `seq(nrow(iris))`. You may want to print the Species using an `as.character()` function, because it's a factor variable by default.

7. `While`: Set `i = 12`. While `i > 0`, print out **i is a positive number**, where `i` should be the number the loop is in.

8. `For` and `if`:
   - For an extra challenge, first declare four `NULL` objects, `Diet1` through `Diet4`.
   - Use a `for` loop to loop through all the rows of `ChickWeight`. If the chick's diet is `Diet1`, add that row to `Diet1` using the `rbind()` function. You should use `rbind(Diet1, that row of ChickWeight)`.
   - Then, check to see whether you got only the correct chicks in each dataset by viewing them.

This is by no means the best way of creating these four datasets, but it is an interesting challenge to think about how loops work.

# Data Import and Export

We've used some of R's built-in datasets so far in this book, but most of the time, data scientists will have to import and export data that comes from external sources in and out of R. Data can come and go in many different forms, and while we'll not cover them all here, we'll touch on some of the most common forms.

Data import and export are truly one subsection in R, because most of the time, the functions are opposites: for example, `read.csv()` takes in the character string name of a `.csv` file, and you save the output as a dataset in your environment, while `write.csv()` takes in the name of the dataset in your environment and the character string name of a file to write to.

There are built-in functions in R for the data import and export of many common file types, such as `read.table()` for `.txt` files, `read.csv()` for `.csv` files, and `read.delim()` for other types of delimited files (such as tab or | delimited, where | is the pipe operator appropriated as a separator). For pretty much any other file type, you have to use a package, usually one written for the import of that particular file type. Common data import packages for other types of data, such as SAS, Excel, SPSS, or Stata data, include the packages `readr`, `haven`, `xlsx`, `Hmisc`, and `foreign`:

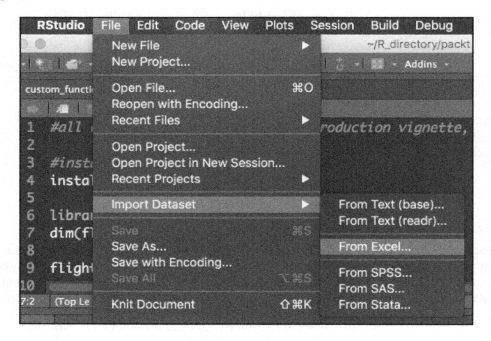

RStudio also has point and click methods for importing data. If you navigate to **File | Import Dataset**, you'll see that you have six options:

- **From text (base)**
- **From text (readr)**
- **From Excel**
- **From SPSS**
- **From SAS**
- **From Stata**

These options call the required packages and functions that are necessary to input data of that type into R. The packages and functions are listed in order, as follows:

- `base::read.table()`
- `readr::read_* functions`
- `xlsx::read_excel()`
- `haven::read_sav()`
- `haven::read_sas()`
- `haven::read_dta()`

One advantage of loading data using one of these functions is that you can see the **Import Text Data** window. This window allows you to toggle different options, such as what to **Name** the dataset once it's imported, which **Delimiter** is used, how many rows to **Skip**, what value to use for missing data, and more. There's also a **Code Preview**, which allows you to see what the code will look like when you import your data. The following screenshot displays this:

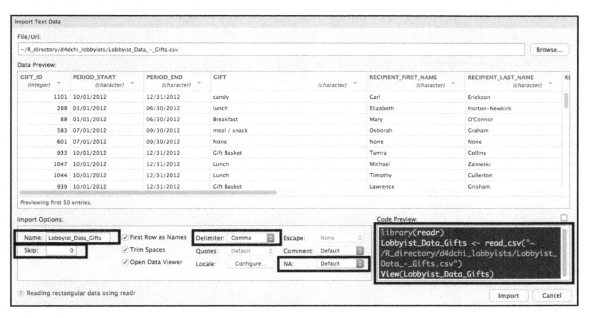

To use most of these functions, you must follow these basic steps:

1. Figure out what type of data you're dealing with—is it a CSV? Is it from SAS? and so on.
2. Find the appropriate function to import that type of data.
3. The first (and sometimes only argument) to the function is a character string indicating where that data is located on your computer.
4. If applicable, tweak the settings of the appropriate function, such as indicating the separator with `sep` or setting `stringAsFactors`.

 A synthetic dataset of 20 students, including their height in inches, weight in pounds, hair color, eye color, and United States' men's shoe sizes has been uploaded to the repository on GitHub, and can be found at the following URL: `https://github.com/TrainingByPackt/R-Programming-Fundamentals/tree/master/lesson1`.

Synthetic data means it was created for the purposes of this exercise and is not a dataset collected from an experiment. The dataset is saved in three formats:

- Text-delimited `.txt` file
- comma-separated values `.csv` file
- Microsof Excel worksheet `.xlsx` file

We'll be downloading all three of these directly from GitHub and importing them into RStudio. To do so, we'll need to use the URL, as a character string, as the first argument to all of the functions we'll use to import data.

 When downloading data from GitHub directly, be sure you've clicked to view the **Raw** version of the dataset, as shown in the following screenshot:

We can import data directly from GitHub by using the `read.table()` function. If we input the URL where the dataset is stored, the function will download it for you, as shown in the following example:

```
students_text <- read.table("https://raw.githubusercontent.com/
TrainingByPackt/R-Programming-Fundamentals/master/lesson1/students.txt")
```

While this code will read in the table, if we open and examine it, we will notice that the variable names are currently the first row of the dataset. To find the options for `read.table()`, we can use the following command:

```
?read.table
```

Reading the documentation, it says that the default value for the header argument is FALSE. If we set it to TRUE, `read.table()` will know that our table contains—as the first row—the variable names, and they should be read in as names. Here is the example:

```
students_text <- read.table("https://raw.githubusercontent.com/
TrainingByPackt/-Programming-Fundamentals/master/lesson1/students.
txt",header = TRUE)
```

The data has now been imported correctly, with the variable names in the correct place.

We may want to convert the `Height_inches` variable to centimeters and the `Weight_ lbs` variable to kilograms. We can do so with the following code:

```
students_text$Height_cm <- (students_text$Height_inches * 2.54)
students_text$Weight_kg <- (students_text$Weight_lbs / 0.453592)
```

Since we've added these two variables, it may now be necessary to export the table out of R, perhaps to email it to a colleague for their use or to re-upload it on GitHub. The opposite of `read.table()` is `write.table()`. Take a look at the following example:

```
write.table(students_text, "students_text_out.txt")
```

This will write out the `students_text` dataset we're using in R to a file called `students_text_out` in our working directory folder on our machine.

There are additional options for `read.table()` that we could use as well. We can actually import a `.csv` file this way by setting the `sep` argument equal to a comma. We can skip rows with `skip = some number`, and add our own row names or column names by passing in a vector of either of those to the `row.names` or `col.names` argument.

Most of the other data import and export functions in R work much like `read.table()` and `write.table()`. Let's import the students' data from the `.csv` format, which can be done in three different ways, using `read.table()`, `read.csv()`, and `read_csv()`.

1. Import the `students.csv` file from GitHub using `read.table()`. Save it as a dataset called `students_csv1`, using the following code:

   ```
   students_csv1 <-read.table("https://raw.githubusercontent.com/
   TrainingByPackt/R-Programming-Fundamentals/master/lesson1/students.
   csv", header = TRUE, sep = ",")
   ```

2. Import `students.csv` using `read.csv()`, which works very similar to `read.table()`:

   ```
   students_csv2 <- read.csv("https://raw.githubusercontent.com/
   TrainingByPackt/R-Programming-Fundamentals/master/lesson1/students.
   csv")
   ```

3. Download the `readr` package:

   ```
   install.packages("readr")
   ```

4. Load the `readr` package:

   ```
   library(readr)
   ```

5. Import `students.csv` using `read_csv()`:

   ```
   students_csv3 <- read_csv("https://raw.githubusercontent.com/
   TrainingByPackt/R-Programming-Fundamentals/master/lesson1/students.
   csv")
   ```

6. Examine `students_csv2` and `students_csv3` with `str()`:

   ```
   str(students_csv2)
   str(students_csv3)
   ```

**Output**:

The output for the `str(students_csv2)` function is as follows:

```
'data.frame': 20 obs. of 5 variables:
$ Height_inches: int 65 55 60 61 62 66 69 54 57 58 ...
$ Weight_lbs: int 120 135 166 154 189 200 250 122 101 178 ...
$ EyeColor: Factor w/ 4 levels "Blue","Brown",...: 1 2 4 2 3 3 1 1 1 2 ...
$ HairColor: Factor w/ 4 levels "Black","Blond",...: 3 2 1 3 2 4 4 3 3 1 ...
$ USMensShoeSize: int 9 5 6 7 8 9 10 5 6 4 ...
```

The output for the `str(students_csv3)` function is as follows:

```
Classes 'tbl_df', 'tbl' and 'data.frame': 20 obs. of 5 variables:
$ Height_inches : int 65 55 60 61 62 66 69 54 57 58 ...
$ Weight_lbs : int 120 135 166 154 189 200 250 122 101 178 ...
$ EyeColor : chr "Blue" "Brown" "Hazel" "Brown" ... $ HairColor : chr "Brown"
"Blond" "Black" "Brown" ...
$ USMensShoeSize: int 9 5 6 7 8 9 10 5 6 4 ...
```

A few notes about the three different ways we read in the `.csv` file in the exercise are as follows:

- `read.table()`, with `header = TRUE` and `sep = ","` reads the data in correctly
- For `read.csv()`, the header argument is `TRUE` by default, so we don't have to specify it:
  - If we view the dataset, using `str(students_csv2)`, we can see that the `HairColor` and `EyeColor` variables got read in as factor variables by default
  - This is because the `stringsAsFactors` option is `TRUE` by default for `read.csv()`
- For `read_csv()` in the `readr` package, the opposite is true about the default `stringsAsFactors` value; it is now `FALSE`:
  - Therefore, `HairColor` and `EyeColor` are read in as character variables. You can verify this with `str(students_csv3)`
  - If we wanted factor variables, would have to change the variables ourselves after import or set `stringsAsFactors = TRUE` to automatically import all character variables as factors, as in `read.csv()`

# Excel Spreadsheets

One last common data type is Microsoft Excel spreadsheets, which are usually saved with the file extension .xlsx. We can use the xlsx R library, which contains read. xlsx() to import the students.xlsx file from GitHub. There's only one sheet in this file, but if there was more than one, we could specify which sheet to read in with the sheet argument.

Let's now use the xlsx package to import and export Microsoft Excel spreadsheet data. Follow the steps given below:

1. Navigate to the .xlsx version of the students dataset on GitHub, at the following link: https://github.com/TrainingByPackt/R-Programming-Fundamentals/blob/master/lesson1/students.xlsx.

2. Hit **View Raw** and it will automatically download to your computer.

3. Move the file from your **Downloads** folder to the working directory folder on your computer.

4. Install and load the xlsx package by using the following code:

```
install.packages("openxlsx")
library(openxlsx)
```

5. Import students.csv using read.xlsx():

```
students_xlsx <- read.xlsx("students.xlsx")
```

6. Create a new variable in students_xlsx, called id, with the following code:

```
students_xlsx$id <- seq(1:nrow(students_xlsx))
```

7. Export students_xlsx to your working directory:

```
write.xlsx(students_xlsx, "students_xlsx_out.xlsx")
```

8. Optionally, if you have a program installed on your machine that will open
   .xlsx files, open students_xlsx_out.xlsx and check to see whether the id
   variable exists.

> If, instead of importing data directly from GitHub, you are looking to
> import data stored on your computer, do the following: Save the data in
> your working directory. Remember that this is the folder you've chosen to
> save your project in, which you can double check with getwd():
> ```
> > getwd()
> [1] "/Users/kaelenmedeiros/R_directory/packt_introDSR/BeginningDSwRCodeFiles"
> ```

9. As you import data, the first argument will be the name of the dataset as a
   character string (instead of the URLs we'll use throughout this chapter). For
   example, if students.txt was saved on your computer, you could import it
   with read_table("students.txt").

In your work as a data scientist, there are a few common data types you may encounter.
The following table provides common data file types and explains how to import and
export them in R:

| File Type | Delimiter/Origin of dataset | function(s) to import data (package name) | function(s) to export data (package name) |
|---|---|---|---|
| .csv, CSV | comma | read.csv (base), read_csv (readr) | write.csv (base), write_csv (readr) |
| depends (.txt, .csv) | tab | read.table, with sep = "\t" | write.table, with sep = "/t" |
| .xlsx | Excel sheet | read.xlsx (xlsx) | write.xlsx (xlsx) |
| .sav | SPSS | spss.get (Hmisc), read_sav (haven) | not advisable |
| .sas7bdat | SAS | sasxport.get (Hmisc), read_sas (haven) | not advisable |
| .dta | STATA | read.dta (foreign), read_ dta (haven) | not advisable |

These are, of course, not the only file types you can read in and out. R can read in data from
everything listed, plus from other web datasets (a URL file), from SQL databases, JSON
files, XML files, shapefiles for creating maps, and more. There are quite a few data types
that R can use to handle importing, and usually a package is already written for doing so.

# Activity: Exporting and Importing the mtcars Dataset

### Scenario

You have been asked to calculate a new variable in the mtcars built-in dataset and export the data so that you can email it to a colleague.

### Aim

To export a dataset to a .csv file, edit it, and import it back into R using the appropriate functions.

### Prerequisites

You must have R and RStudio installed on machine. Notepad, MS Excel, or any other program that can open .txt and .csv files will also be helpful.

### Steps for Completion

1. Open a new R Script and save it as a file called lesson1_activityD.R.
2. Load the datasets library, and then the mtcars dataset.
3. Create a variable called hpcyl equal to the horsepower per cylinders of each car.
4. Write mtcars into a .csv file called mtcars_out.csv.
5. Read the dataset back in and call it mtcars_in by using read.csv().

 Do you have to set the header or the stringsAsFactors argument? If you can't remember, check by typing ?read.csv into your console.

# Getting Help with R

We've covered a lot in this chapter, and this is the last thing that you'll carry throughout this book and into the rest of the time you spend learning R: how do you get help with R programming and data science?

# Package Documentation and Vignettes

One advantage of using R is that it is a very well-documented programming language. This is often because there is a certain amount of documentation that is required by CRAN before it will publish a package on the website.

It is considered a best practice to document your packages or functions well, no matter where you are publishing them. Good documentation is important, both for other people who may use your functions and also for yourself when you return to them in the future.

As such, there are a few built-in ways in R to get help. The first way to get help is to use the package documentation. You can access it by using the help() function or the question mark ?. These will do the same thing. For example, say you (this one happens a lot) can't remember off the top of your head the inputs to the glm() function. The following code will bring up the documentation for the glm() function, as shown in the following screenshot:

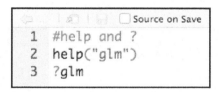

If you read the documentation, you will see that you need to input at least a formula, family, and dataset name.

Of course, help() and the question mark ? can only help you with packages and functions you already know the name of. When you're not as sure, you can use help. search() and ?? to find things. These functions are also analogous, and will search the built-in help documentation for any and all instances of what you're looking for, for example, help.search("logit") or ??logit.

Both of the preceding options return a long list of help pages where `logit` appears. As you look through the results of your search for `logit` in the R documentation, you may notice that there are lots of things written in the format `agricolae::reg.homog` and `base::Control`.

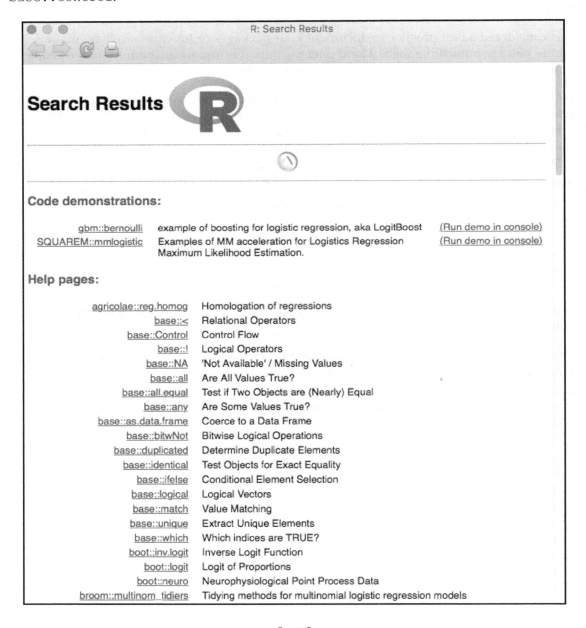

In R, this notation means that the `agricolae` package has a function called `reg.homog` (`agricolae::reg.homog`), and that the base package has a function called `Control` (`base::Control`).

 The double colon :: always separates a package and function name in R. (This comes in handy when you have functions named after the same thing in multiple packages, such as `stats::filter` and `dplyr::filter`!)

In addition to the often very helpful and thorough documentation built into R, some packages also have one or more vignettes, which are documents written by the author(s) of the package that are intended to demonstrate the main functionality of the functions contained in the package. You can bring these up inside RStudio in a number of ways.

Let's use the vignette-related functions `browseVignettes()` and `vignettes()` to explore the vignettes for R packages. Follow the steps given below:

1. To see a list of many available vignettes in R, use the `browseVignettes()` method:
     - Browse the vignettes available for the `dplyr` package using the method syntax `browseVignettes(package = "dplyr")` or `browseVignettes("dplyr")`

2. Access the vignette for the `tibble` package using the syntax `vignette("tibble")` or `vignette(package = "tibble")`.

3. In a search engine of your choice, find the vignette for the R package `tidyr`.

Check your **Help** tab to see the vignettes when you access them inside of RStudio. The output will be as follows:

---

# Tibbles

Tibbles are a modern take on data frames. They keep the features that have stood the test of time, and drop the features that used to be convenient but are now frustrating (i.e. converting character vectors to factors).

## Creating

`tibble()` is a nice way to create data frames. It encapsulates best practices for data frames:

- It never changes an input's type (i.e., no more `stringsAsFactors = FALSE`!).

```
tibble(x = letters)
#> # A tibble: 26 x 1
#>     x
#>     <chr>
#> 1 a
#> 2 b
#> 3 c
#> 4 d
#> # ... with 22 more rows
```

This makes it easier to use with list-columns:

```
tibble(x = 1:3, y = list(1:5, 1:10, 1:20))
#> # A tibble: 3 x 2
#>       x y
#>     <int> <list>
#> 1     1 <int [5]>
#> 2     2 <int [10]>
#> 3     3 <int [20]>
```

List-columns are most commonly created by `do()`, but they can be useful to create by hand.

- It never adjusts the names of variables:

```
names(data.frame(`crazy name` = 1))
#> [1] "crazy.name"
names(tibble(`crazy name` = 1))
```

---

# Activity: Exploring the Introduction to dplyr Vignette

## Scenario

You have been asked to write code by utilizing the main verb functions (`filter`, `arrange`, `select`, `mutate`, and `summarise`) that are available in the `dplyr` package.

## Aim

To gain experience of looking for vignettes and to also introduce the `dplyr` package.

## Prerequisites

A web browser capable of looking at an R package vignette.

## Steps for Completion

1. Navigate, in your web browser, to the introduction to the `dplyr` vignette (`https://cran.r-project.org/web/packages/dplyr/vignettes/dplyr.html`). `dplyr` is a package that is part of the `Tidyverse` we installed way back in the first section. You can also access the vignette inside of RStudio by running `vignette("dplyr")` in a script or by typing it in the console. It will appear in the **Help** tab in the lower right window.

2. Open up a new R Script (**File | New File | R Script**). Save it as a file called `dplyr_vignette_walkthrough.R`.

3. Read the `dplyr` vignette, running at least the first line of code for each of the main five `dplyr` verbs (`filter`, `arrange`, `select`, `mutate`, and `summarise`). Make sure that your output mirrors that of the vignette.

4. Stop when you reach the heading **Patterns of operations**, about halfway down the page. (It is recommended that you return later and read the entire vignette, as the `dplyr` package is very useful.)

5. If you have time, play with the `dplyr` code a bit and try to understand more about how the main five verbs work through experimentation.

# RStudio Community, Stack Overflow, and the Rest of the Web

Two of the main community-based resources online are the official RStudio Community and Stack Overflow.

**Stack Overflow (SO)** `https://stackoverflow.com/` is a fantastic resource for a variety of questions relating to technology, with no limit on the different kinds of programming languages or analysis types you can ask questions about—the sky's the limit! There is an r tag (`https://stackoverflow.com/questions/tagged/r`) that has, as of late March 2018, 230,000+ tagged questions in it. Often, the best way to find what you're looking for is to go to a search engine, type something along the lines of how to relevel a factor in r, and often a SO post (or even multiple!) will be the top hits.

The RStudio Community (`https://community.rstudio.com/`) website is a forum that's run by RStudio themselves. It is expected that questions will be R-focused. They are often answered by the very people who wrote the packages and functions you are asking questions about. Questions are tagged by category, such as **RMarkdown**, **General**, and **tidyverse**, to help you navigate. The forum is searchable and filterable, and is a great place to get answers to any R-related questions.

More generally, **#rstats** on twitter (`https://twitter.com/search?q=%23rstatssrc=typd`) is a great place to go for R questions, tips and tricks, and to find a community of people who are all over the R usage spectrum, from beginners to seasoned pros, who have often developed the packages used in R every day. Many R experts check the **#rstats** hashtag for questions, so it's another great way to get answers to R and data science queries. It's also a great way to find blog posts about R, which often include worked out examples that someone has solved, which are often useful as you are learning.

As learners new to R, you're sure to have many questions as you move on in your journey. Hopefully, you now know about and are even beginning to get comfortable with the many places both built into R and on the internet that you can go to for help, and eventually even help others as you gain confidence and skills.

# Summary

We've covered a lot in this introductory chapter and have plenty more to do, but don't fret! We'll continue to use plenty of examples and activities throughout to help you remember what we're learning. Let's press forward on to the next chapter, where we'll begin to look at some data more closely and do some cleaning and data management, which is necessary to get us one step closer to modeling and analysis.

# 2

# Data Visualization and Graphics

Data visualizations are very important in data science. They are used as a part of
**Exploratory Data Analysis (EDA)**, to familiarize yourself with data, to examine the
distributions of variables, to identify outliers, and to help guide data cleaning and analysis.
They are also used to communicate results to a variety of audiences, from other data
scientists to customers.

EDA is the general name for the process of using numerical summaries,
plots, and aggregating methods to explore a dataset to familiarize yourself
with its contents. It will almost certainly involve you examining the
distribution of variables in the dataset, looking at missingness, deciding
whether there are any outliers or errors, and generally getting a feel for
what is contained in your data.

In this chapter, you'll learn about base plots, ggplot2, and will be briefly introduced to more
advanced plotting with the applications Shiny and Plotly.

By the end of this chapter, you will be able to:

- Use Base R for plotting, and identify when to do so
- Create a variety of different data visualizations using the ggplot2 package
- Explain different tools for interactive plotting in R

# Creating Base Plots

R can plot data without installing any additional packages. This is commonly referred to as **base plotting**. It is called base plotting because, like functions that come pre-installed with R in the base package, discussed in `Chapter 1`, *Introduction to R*, these plots are built into R. The graphics package comes with a download of R and enables you to plot data without installing any other packages.

 To see details on the graphics package, you can search for *R graphics package* in a search engine of your choice or navigate to the following URL: `https://stat.ethz.ch/R-manual/R-devel/library/graphics/html/00Index.html`.

Base plots are often not used outside of work done for data cleaning and EDA. Many data scientists use other more *aesthetically pleasing plots*, such as those generated using ggplot2 or Plotly, for any plots or graphs that a customer may see. It is important to know how to use `plot()` and create base plots, however, so let's dive in!

# The plot() Function

```
main

        an overall title for the plot: see title.

sub

        a sub title for the plot: see title.

xlab

        a title for the x axis: see title.

ylab

        a title for the y axis: see title.

asp

        the y/x aspect ratio, see plot.window.
```

The `plot()` function is the backbone of base plots in R. It provides capability for generic X-Y plotting. It requires only one argument, *x*, which should be something to plot—a vector of numbers, one variable of a dataset, or a model object such as linear or logistic regression. You can, of course, add a second variable, *y*, plus an assortment of options to customize the plot, but *x* is the only input required for the function to run successfully.

For anything beyond the basic *x* and *y* arguments to the function, you'll need to get very familiar with using `?plot` or `help(plot)`. The documentation suggests options, such as those for titles and axis labels, and also points you to the documentation for other graphical parameters, found under the `par()` function in R. The options provided by the function are far more detailed and allow you to change the colors, fonts, positions of axis labels, and much more for your base plots.

Beyond knowing the basics about how to use `plot()`, you do not need to memorize all of the function's possible options. Realistically, you do not need to memorize all of the options for any function in R. Most of the time when you are doing your work, you will have access to documentation and help. Learning R is about learning both how to use functions and also how to look for help when you need it.

All of the preceding options take you directly to the help documentation, also found online at the following URL: `https://stat.ethz.ch/R-manual/R-devel/library/graphics/html/plot.html`.

When you start out to write plots in base R, you may be interested to know that there are many other inputs besides just the data you want to plot. You can access the R help documentation for the `plot()` function in the following ways:

- `?plot`
- `help("plot")`
- `help(plot)`

In RStudio, sometimes the plot may be skewed or squished, as it is constrained by the size of your plot window (usually the bottom-right window, under the **Plots** tab.) You can, at any time, click the **Zoom** button and your plot will pop out, usually larger, and give you a better look:

If we first load the datasets library, we gain access to a number of built-in datasets in R that will be useful for both base plotting and using ggplot2. To begin with, we'll use the mtcars dataset. mtcars is a very famous example dataset, and its description (accessed using ?mtcars) is as follows:

> *The data was extracted from the 1974 Motor Trend US magazine, and comprises fuel consumption and 10 aspects of automobile design and performance for 32 automobiles (1973–74 models).*

Minimally, we can plot just one variable of mtcars, for example mpg or the miles per gallon of the cars. This generates a very basic plot of mpg on the y-axis, with index on the x-axis, literally corresponding to the row index of each observation, as follows:

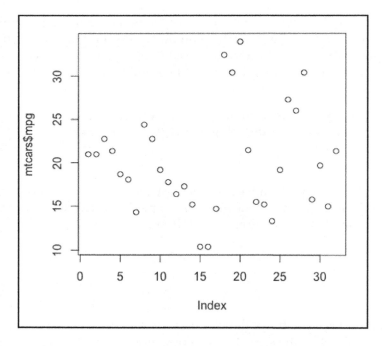

This plot isn't very informative, but it is powerful in terms of seeing how well R can plot even when it is not installed on a particular machine. Let's add in a second variable and plot mpg versus wt:

```
plot(mtcars$wt, mtcars$mpg)
```

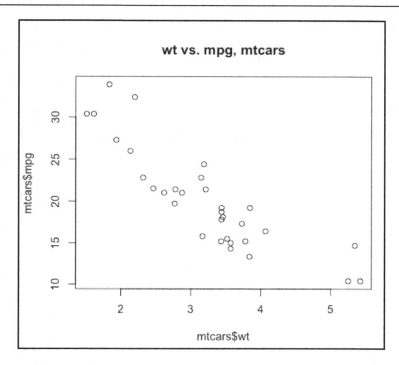

If we plot `mpg` versus `wt` (*y* vs. *x*), we can see a clear negative linear trend, that is, when the weight increases, the miles per gallon decreases. This isn't terribly unexpected—heavier cars will require more gas to operate and will therefore get less miles to the gallon.

You should also notice that the default axis labels are the variables exactly as input into `plot()` (so, `mtcars$wt` and `mtcars$mpg` include the dataset name and dollar sign to access each variable). There is no title by default, and the default shape is an open circle.

These last two plots were an example of what happens if you input variables from a dataset into `plot()`. The `plot()` function is very versatile, however, and you can input a number of different things and still create base plots. Let's discuss a few of the options in the next few subtopics.

## Factor Variables

We input a few variables from `mtcars` into `plot()`, but they were continuous. What happens if, instead, we input a factor variable?

For example, the `cyl` variable in `mtcars` gives the number of cylinders each car has. If we input it as a factor variable into `plot`, we get a bar chart (histogram) by default, where each bar gives a count of how many cars have each number of cylinders:

```
plot(as.factor(mtcars$cyl))
```

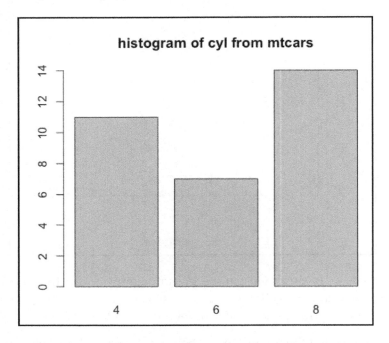

Let's now create plots using factor variables and learn to differentiate between plots created with factor variables and those created without. Follow the steps given below:

1. Load the `mtcars` dataset using the `data("mtcars")` method.
2. Plot the gear variable of `mtcars` without changing it to a factor variable using `plot(mtcars$gear)`. What kind of plot do you get?
3. Now, plot the gear variable of `mtcars` as a factor variable, as follows:

```
plot(as.factor(mtcars$gear))
```

What kind of plot is generated?

**Output**: The following scatterplot is the output we get when the `gear` variable is plotted without changing it to the factor variable:

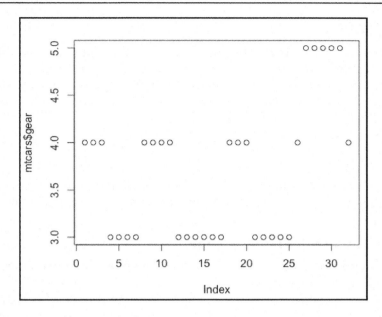

The following histogram/bar chart is the output we get when the `gear` variable is plotted after changing it to the factor variable:

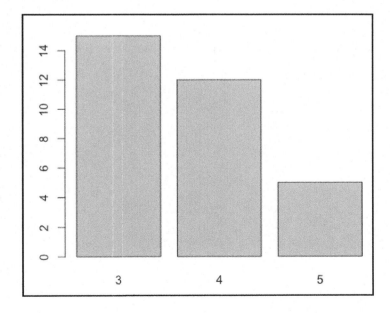

# Model Objects

As we observed in the factor variable example, the function defaults to certain types of plots depending on the kind of data you put into it. If you were to input a linear model object, `plot()` automatically returns four helpful model diagnostic plots, including the Residuals versus Fitted and Normal Q-Q plots, which help you determine whether your model fits well. The following code demonstrates this:

```
mtcars_lm <- lm(mpg ~ wt, data = mtcars)
plot(mtcars_lm)
```

The process of generating all four of these plots is somewhat tedious, however, so instead, let's look at plotting more than one plot at a time, combined with model object plotting.

## Plotting More Than One Plot at a Time

One neat feature in R is that you can plot more than one plot at a time on the same viewing window. Inside of `par()`, if we pass `mfrow = c(rows, cols)`, where `rows` is the number of rows of plots you'd like and `cols` is the number of columns of plots you'd like, you can plot a number of plots on the same screen. If we return to the `mtcars_lm()` example we just covered, we can plot all four model diagnostic plots in the same window by first running the following line of code:

```
par(mfrow = c(2,2))
```

Next, you need to execute the following code:

```
plot(mtcars_lm)
```

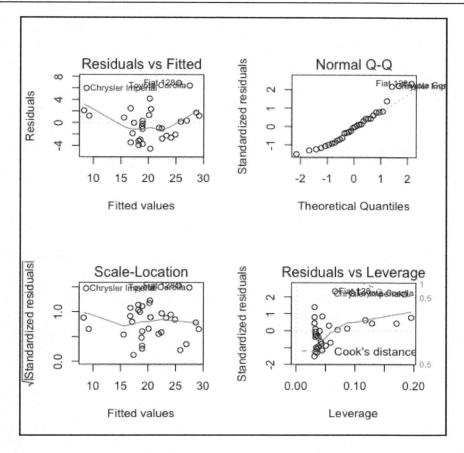

This resets your Global Options in RStudio. So now, every time you try and plot, it will make plots in a *2 × 2* grid. You'll need to reset back to *1 × 1* when you're ready, using either `dev.off()` or simply `par(mfrow = c(1,1))`.

## Creating and Plotting a Linear Model Object

Let's use the function to create a linear model object, and then use `par()`, `mfrow()`, and `plot()` to examine the model diagnostics. Follow the steps given below:

1. Build your own version of `mtcars_lm`, which looks at how the displacement and weight variables affect `mpg` using the following code:

```
mtcars_lm <- lm(mpg ~ disp + wt, data = mtcars)
```

2. Run the following code to enable plotting a 2 × 2 grid of plots so that looking at model diagnostic plots is easier with the following method:

```
par(mfrow = c(2, 2))
```

3. Plot the `mtcars_lm` variable to see the model diagnostic plots using `plot(mtcars_lm)`.

Be sure to turn the 2 × 2 grid off. This will make the plot disappear, so be sure you're done looking at it before you run this line.

4. Turn the 2 × 2 grid off using `dev.off()`.

**Output**: The following is the output we get when we execute the `plot()` function as mentioned in *Step 3*.

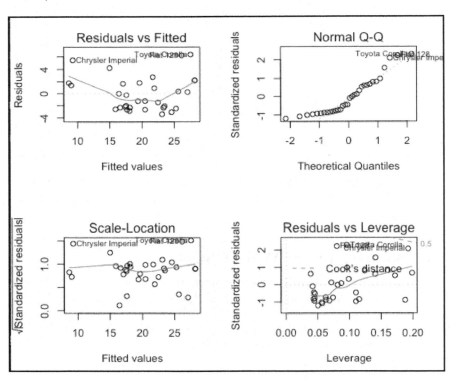

# Titles and Axis Labels

If we want to add a title and custom axis labels to a base plot, it is simply a matter of adding extra inputs to `plot()`. If you examine the documentation for `plot()` using `?plot` or `help(plot)`, you'll see that plot can take a number of inputs that will do the following:

- `main`, for plot titles
- `sub`, for subtitles
    - These will be smaller than the title
    - Subtitles are printed at the bottom of the plot, beneath the x-axis label
- `xlab`, to change the x-axis label
    - By default, the x-axis label will be the name of the variable you input as it is named in the dataset. Use xlab to change it.
- `ylab`, to change the y-axis label
    - The y-axis defaults are the same as for the x-axis, and ylab works just as xlab does.

Let's return to our `mtcars` scatterplot, add a title and subtitle, and also change the axis labels with the following code:

```
plot(mtcars$wt, mtcars$mpg,
    main = "MPG vs. Weight",
    sub = "mtcars dataset",
    xlab = "Weight",
    ylab = "MPG")
```

This adds our title and overrides the default behavior of printing axis labels, which are exactly what was input for *x* and *y*. The plot now has some context in the form of these titles and labels, and is far more understandable, as shown in the following screenshot:

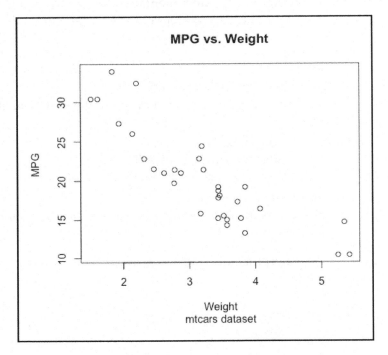

Let's now add titles and axis labels to base plots and utilize the `main`, `sub`, `xlab`, and `ylab` options to change the titles and axis labels of base plots. Follow the steps given below:

1. Load the `iris` dataset using `data("iris")`.
2. Plot petal length and width from the `iris` dataset to see what the plot looks like, and take note of the default axis labels as follows:

```
plot(iris$Petal.Length, iris$Petal.Width)
```

3. Now, add a title, subtitle, and custom axis labels to the same plot using the following code:

```
plot(iris$Petal.Length, iris$Petal.Width,
     main = "Petal Width vs. Length",
     sub = "iris dataset",
     xlab = "Petal Length",
     ylab = "Petal Width")
```

**Output**: The following is the output we get when we execute the code line mentioned in *Step 2*:

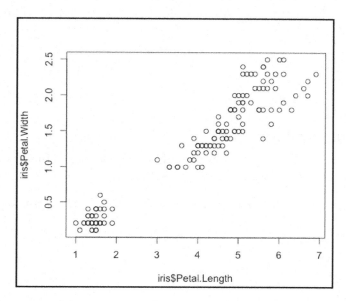

The following is the output we get when we execute the code mentioned in *Step 3*:

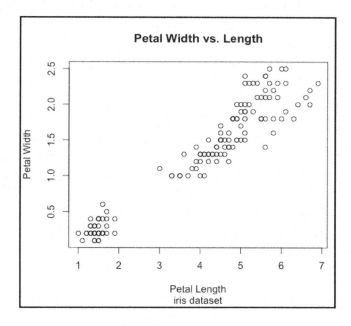

If we decide we'd like to plot in a different color, say red, it's as simple as passing `col = "red"` into `plot()`. R supports the names of many different colors along with hexadecimal color codes. The code to change the previous plot to red would be as follows:

```
plot(mtcars$wt, mtcars$mpg,
     main = "mpg vs. wt, mtcars data",
     xlab = "weight",
     ylab = "mpg",
     col = "red")
```

## Changing the Color of Base Plots

Let's see how you can use the `col` option provided by the `plot()` function to change a plot into a few different colors. Follow the steps given below:

1. Use the `col` option to turn the plot from the last exercise blue as follows:

```
plot(iris$Petal.Length, iris$Petal.Width,
     main = "Petal Width vs. Length",
     sub = "iris dataset",
     xlab = "Petal Length",
     ylab = "Petal Width",
     col = "blue")
```

2. Use the `col` option to turn the plot from the last exercise yellow using the hexadecimal color code `111111`:

```
plot(iris$Petal.Length, iris$Petal.Width,
     main = "Petal Width vs. Length",
     sub = "iris dataset",
     xlab = "Petal Length",
     ylab = "Petal Width",
     col = "111111")
```

**Output:**

1. Check your **Plot** window after executing the code in *Step 1* to be sure that the plot is now blue.
2. Check your **Plot** window after executing the code in *Step 2* to be sure that the plot is now yellow.

It is important to know and understand plot(), as base plots are adequate and useful. However, the ggplot2 package has really taken over the R graphics landscape, and as such we won't spend much more time on base plots. Let's do a quick activity just to be sure we have the hang of them.

# Activity: Recreating Plots with Base Plot Methods

## Scenario

You have been asked to create some base plots that provide information on the mtcars and iris datasets for a junior colleague.

## Prerequisites

Make sure you have R and RStudio installed on your machine.

## Aim

To use plot() by recreating different plots with different base plot methods.

## Steps for completion

1. Load the datasets library using library(datasets).
2. Load the iris and mpg datasets. You will need to make individual calls, using data("mtcars"), for example. You will then see the dataset in your environment as a promise. It will appear as a dataset in your list of datasets in the upper-right window when you first attempt to use it.

3. Recreate the following base plots using `iris` data:
   1. A scatterplot to plot petal width without axis labels:

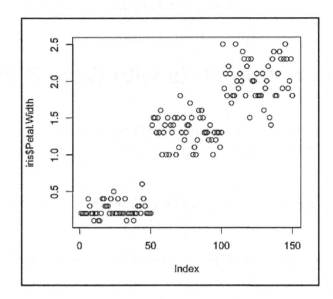

   2. A scatterplot to plot petal length and width with axis labels:

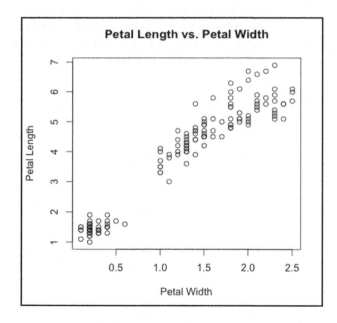

3.  Scatterplots in *1* × *2* grids to plot petal length and width with axis labels:

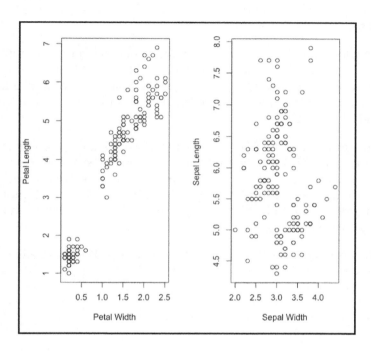

4.  Recreate the following histogram using `mtcars` data to plot the number of cylinders in the color blue:

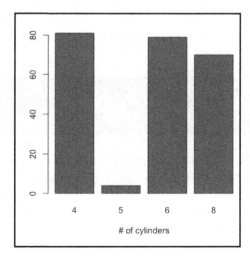

# ggplot2

ggplot2 is an incredibly popular graphics package in R. It can be installed on its own or comes as part of the `Tidyverse` set of packages.

 Developed by Hadley Wickham and Winston Chang, ggplot2 implements the *Grammar of Graphics*, a pre-existing idea in statistical computing, for R. As we begin making plots with ggplot2, you may recognize the aesthetic of the plots, as ggplots are widely used in publications, data journalism, and blog posts.

When you're using ggplot2, both as you're learning how to use it and even when you're more seasoned, the official RStudio ggplot2 cheat sheet will be a resource you may want to keep close for your reference. It will not only remind you of the basics (and more advanced implementations) of how to use ggplot2, it gives suggestions for which plots to use when you have certain types of variables (for example, if you have one continuous variable, you can build a histogram using `geom_hist()`).

 The ggplot2 cheat sheet can be found at the following URL: `https://www.rstudio.com/wp-content/uploads/2015/03/ggplot2-cheatsheet.pdf`. RStudio has also made many different cheat sheets available for common R packages. They can be found on their official website at the following URL: `https://www.rstudio.com/resources/cheatsheets/`.

First and foremost, you'll need to install ggplot2 using `install.packages("ggplot2")` or through point-and-click methods. Then, when you load ggplot2 in RStudio using `library(ggplot2)`, it immediately suggests the ggplot2 **Stack Overflow** tag as a good place to go for any help you might need ggplotting. Recall that we learned about Stack Overflow in `Chapter 1`, *Introduction to R*, as a valuable resource for seeking assistance with R:

```
> library(ggplot2)
Stackoverflow is a great place to get help:
http://stackoverflow.com/tags/ggplot2.
```

 The online documentation for ggplot at the `Tidyverse` website is thorough and can be used to supplement the built-in documentation. The URL is as follows: `http://ggplot2.tidyverse.org/index.html`. It contains many examples and thorough explanations of every element of ggplot2 and is maintained by the authors of the package.

# ggplot2 Basics

To begin with, here is the exact same data, plotted both with `plot()` and `ggplot()`, respectively:

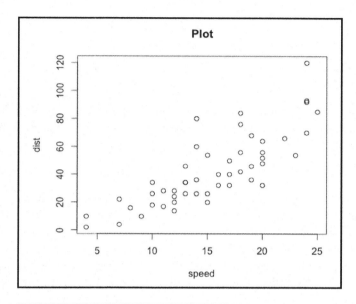

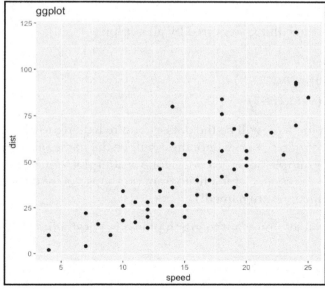

This is the built-in `cars` dataset, which contains only two variables, `speed` and `dist`. You can generate these plots yourself, as follows:

- Plot 1:

  ```
  plot(cars)
  ```

- Plot 2:

  ```
  library(ggplot2)
  ggplot(cars, aes(speed, dist)) + geom_point()
  ```

Voilà! A plot and a ggplot. Which is more aesthetically pleasing to you? Which would you rather publish on a report or your blog? The answer is *probably* the ggplot, if you're like most data scientists out there.

Using ggplot2 requires you to begin to think of each element of a plot as a layer.

First, you have a white screen with only axes defined, two lines symbolizing the *x* and *y* axes. Using the `ggplot()` function, you layer on a dataset that contains what you'll plot and the aesthetics of the plot, defined in the `aes()` function, which corresponds to the things to plot and how to plot them. Then, you layer on a geom, using a `geom_*()` function, which tells ggplot2 what kind of plot you're trying to make. You can layer on additional aesthetics, such as plot titles, axis labels, colors, different point types, and more.

```
ggplot(data = <DATA>) + <GEOM_FUNCTION>(mapping = aes(<MAPPINGS>))
```

In the call, we see the three things required by all ggplots:

1. Dataset (`DATA`)
2. Geom (`GEOM_FUNCTION`)
3. Mappings (`MAPPINGS`)

Your dataset, entered in `DATA`, will be the dataset you're looking to plot variables from. Geoms take the form of `geom_*()`, where the * will be the name of the type of plot you're looking to create, for example `geom_point()` for a scatterplot, `geom_ boxplot()` for a boxplot, and `geom_histogram()` for a histogram (perhaps you're detecting a theme here in how the `geom_*()` functions are named!)

Mappings are the variables you want to graph plus other aesthetics (`aes()` is short for aesthetics)

```
ggplot(data = <DATA>, aes(<GLOBAL MAPPINGS>)) + <GEOM_FUNCTION>(mapping =
aes(<LOCAL MAPPINGS>))
```

Global mappings will apply globally to every layer of your plot. This is a good place to put the variables you'd like to begin plotting and any settings you'd like to apply to everything, for example declaring `alpha = 0.6` here would mean all of your points in a scatterplot are at 60% transparency.

Local mappings will either override or add to any global mappings and apply to that layer only. As you'll see later on, you can include a number of layers in your ggplot (either by plotting multiple variables or by adding layers that include titles or themes, for example), so any local mappings should be applied inside the `geom_*()` or appropriate function (for example, `ggtitle()`).

There are a few things you should know about creating ggplots that will help you along the way. Firstly, you can save a ggplot call and use it for multiple graphs, for example:

```
#save the ggplot data and mappings as 'mtcars_ggplot':
mtcars_ggplot <- ggplot(mtcars, aes(wt, mpg))
#create 2 additional plots:
mtcars_ggplot + geom_point()
mtcars_ggplot + geom_point(aes(col = factor(cyl)))
```

The first line of code saves a ggplot object called `mtcars_ggplot`, which says that you want to use the `mtcars` dataset and the weight (`wt`) and miles per gallon (`mpg`) variables for plotting. This object will be saved in your R environment as a list, and you can view it in the environment by hitting the magnifying glass icon next to its name:

| Name | Type | Value |
|------|------|-------|
| mtcars_ggplot | list [9] (S3: gg, ggplot) | List of length 9 |
| data | list [32 x 11] (S3: data.frame) | A data.frame with 32 rows and 11 columns |
| layers | list [0] | List of length 0 |
| scales | environment [1] (S3: ScalesLis | <environment: 0x108eda358> |
| mapping | list [2] (S3: uneval) | List of length 2 |
| x | symbol | `wt` |
| y | symbol | `mpg` |
| theme | list [0] | List of length 0 |
| coordinates | environment [3] (S3: CoordCa | <environment: 0x108ed8ae8> |
| facet | environment [3] (S3: FacetNul | <environment: 0x108ed76d8> |
| plot_env | environment [4] | <environment: R_GlobalEnv> |
| labels | list [2] | List of length 2 |
| x | character [1] | 'wt' |
| y | character [1] | 'mpg' |

You can see from inside the `mtcars_ggplot` object that it has saved the `mtcars` dataset in the data list. There are currently no layers, because we haven't told it what kind of plot we want yet (or any titles or axis labels). You can see in the mapping list that *x* is now the `wt` variable and *y* is the `mpg` variable, which we indicated by putting those variables in as mapping arguments inside `aes()`. The default labels, which are taken directly from the variable names as they are saved in the dataset, are also listed in the labels list, as *x* = `wt` and *y* = `mpg`, which are both character strings.

The second line of code plots a basic scatterplot of miles per gallon by weight of the car. It calls the `mtcars_ggplot` object for beginning guidance (`DATA` and `MAPPINGS`) and then uses `geom_point()` as its `GEOM`. The third line of code also creates a scatterplot, similarly calling `mtcars_ggplot` as its guide, but adds in an additional local mapping inside `geom_point()`, declaring that it wants the points colored (`col`) by the factor variable `cyl`, which indicates how many cylinders the car has. If you first load `mtcars` in your R environment, if you haven't already, using `data("mtcars")`, all of this code is executable in R. Feel free to try it to see the different plots.

Secondly, the plus signs you'll need to add layers to a `ggplot()` object must *always* come at the end of a line. The following code will run successfully to create the plot we saw at the beginning of this subtopic:

```
ggplot(cars, aes(speed, dist)) + geom_point()
```

The following code will not run, because the plus sign has been moved down to the second line, in front of `geom_point()`:

```
ggplot(cars, aes(speed, dist)) + geom_point()
```

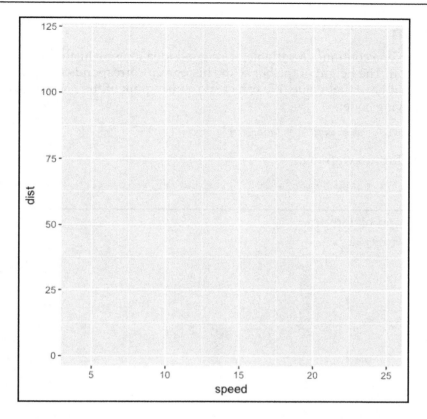

If you attempt to run code with the plus sign at the beginning of a line, preceding `geom_point()`, as in the previous example, a blank plot, as shown in the preceding screenshot, will generate in your **Plots** window in RStudio and you will get the following error in your console:

```
Error in +geom_point() : invalid argument to unary operator
```

Let's walk through some basic types of ggplots using the `mtcars` dataset, which we've used a few times so far and will continue to use throughout the book. Built-in datasets in R are convenient to use for trying to learn new things; plus they can be helpful to use for creating examples for others when we need help with something.

# Histogram

When you have one continuous variable, it's a good idea to use a histogram to get an idea of its distribution. The height of the bar of the histogram corresponds to the number of observations that have that value. We can create a histogram of the mpg variable in mtcars using the following code:

```
ggplot(mtcars, aes(mpg)) + geom_histogram()
```

This code will throw a warning:

```
'stat_bin()' using 'bins = 30'. Pick better value with 'binwidth'.
```

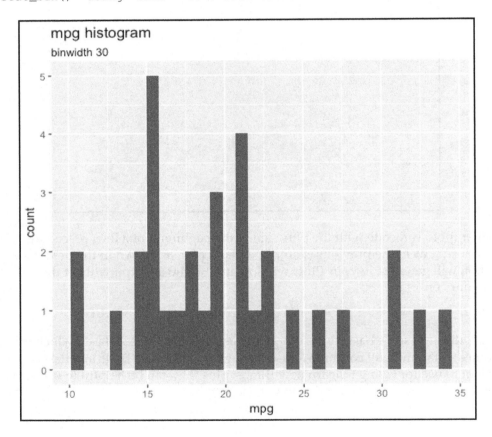

The default number of bins is always 30, and you should always change it and find a better value for your data. The default means that it takes the range of the data (here, `mpg` is between 10.4 and 33.9) and divides it by 30 to create bins—which, in this case, is a bit large, and causes our binwidth to be equal to 0.783, which is tiny! Let's choose a few different bin widths to see what happens. Note that you need to specify binwidth inside of `geom_histogram()` as a local mapping.

`binwidth = 10` gives us almost no detail—we can see three groups of observations of the data:

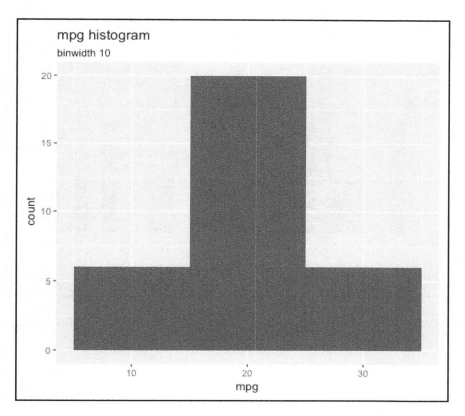

`binwidth = 1` isn't bad, but the graph shows some gaps. Let's see if we can close them:

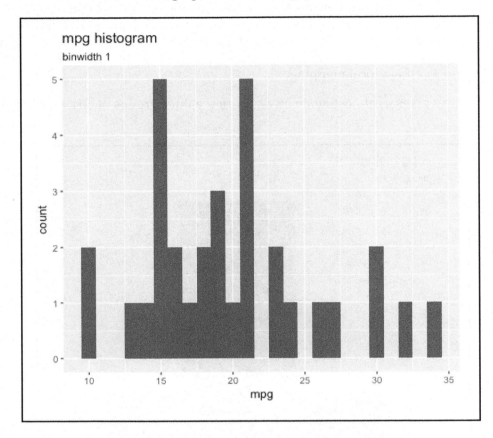

Using a binwidth of 3 shows decent amount of detail, as shown in the following graph:

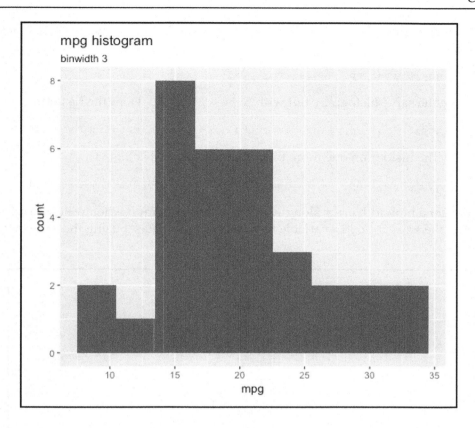

## Creating Histograms using ggplot2

In this section, we will create a histogram with ggplot2 and experiment with different binwidths to find the best representation of the data. Follow the steps below:

1. Install the `ggplot2` library and then load it:

```
install.packages("ggplot2")
library(ggplot2)
```

2. Load the `msleep` dataset, a built-in dataset that comes installed with ggplot2, using `data("msleep")`.

3. Create a histogram of the `sleep_total` variable from `msleep`. Do you get the binwidth error?

```
ggplot(msleep, aes(sleep_total)) + geom_histogram()
```

4. Try the same histogram, but with `binwidth = 10`. Does the histogram improve?

```
ggplot(msleep, aes(sleep_total)) + geom_histogram(binwidth = 10)
```

5. Try the histogram one more time, now with `binwidth = 1`:

```
ggplot(msleep, aes(sleep_total)) + geom_histogram(binwidth = 1)
```

**Output**: We get a binwidth error along with the following graph when we try to create a histogram of the `sleep_total` variable from the `msleep` dataset using the code mentioned in *Step 3*:

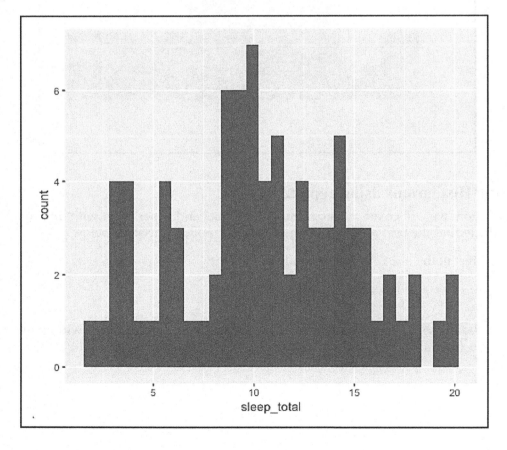

The following is the histogram with `binwidth = 10`:

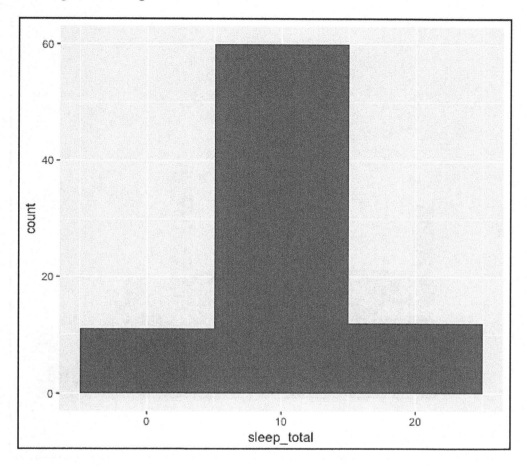

The following is the histogram with `binwidth = 1`:

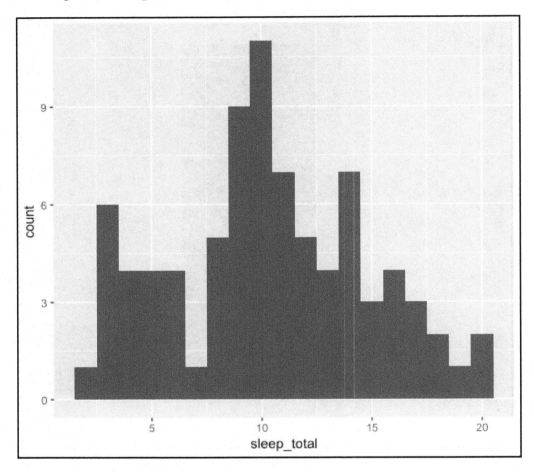

# Bar Chart

For one categorical or factor variable, you can create a bar chart. We can create a bar chart of the `cyl` variable of `mtcars` using the following code:

```
#using geom_bar()
ggplot(mtcars, aes(cyl)) + geom_bar()
```

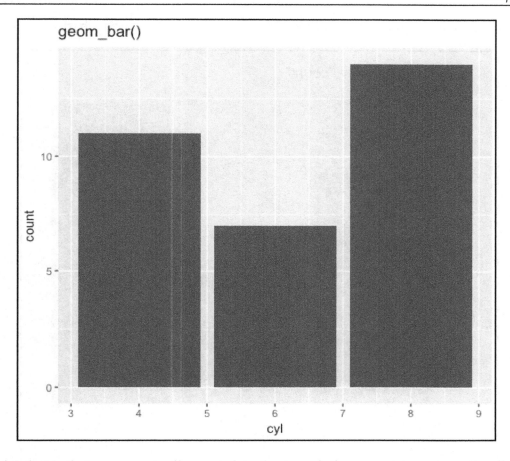

One fun fact is that we can actually create bar charts with the geom_histogram() call as well, by including stat = "count", as follows:

```
#using geom_histogram() and stat
ggplot(mtcars, aes(cyl)) + geom_histogram(stat = "count")
```

You can ignore the warning it will throw; this creates the exact same bar chart:

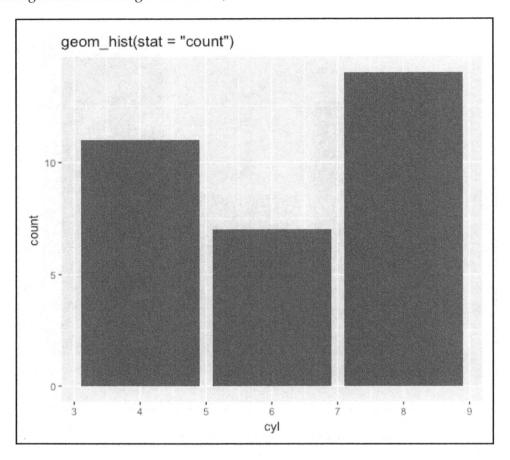

## Creating a Bar Chart with ggplot2 using Two Different Methods

Let's create a bar chart with ggplot2 using both `geom_bar()` and `geom_hist()`.

1. Create a bar chart of the `vore` variable from `msleep` using `geom_bar()`, as follows:

```
ggplot(msleep, aes(vore)) + geom_bar()
```

2. Create the same bar chart of the `vore` variable from `msleep` using `geom_histogram(stat = "count")`, as follows:

```
ggplot(msleep, aes(vore)) + geom_histogram(stat = "count")
```

**Output**: The following is the output we get after executing the code mentioned in *Step 1*:

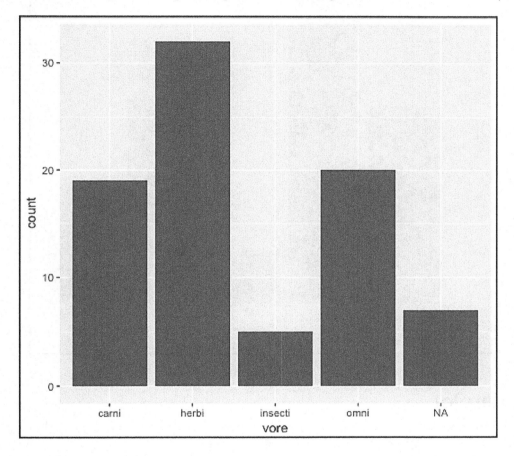

The following is the output we get after executing the code mentioned in *Step 2*:

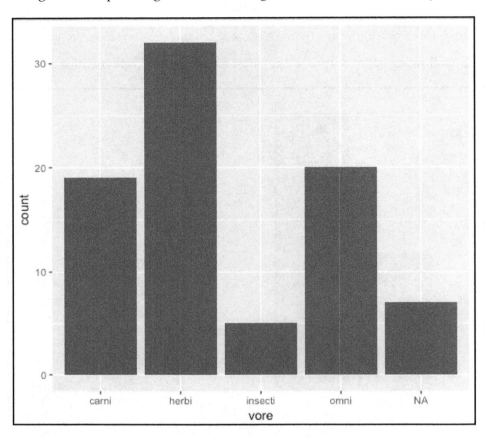

# Scatterplot

Two continuous variables are a good candidate for a scatterplot, which is created using `geom_point()` in ggplot2. You can also create scatterplots using `geom_ jitter()`. Using `jitter` instead of `point` adds a small amount of noise (tiny on the order of decimals) to each observation, spreading them out from one another slightly so they're easier to see.

We can create a scatterplot with the `wt` and `mpg` variables from `mtcars` using the following code:

```
ggplot(mtcars, aes(wt, mpg)) + geom_point()
```

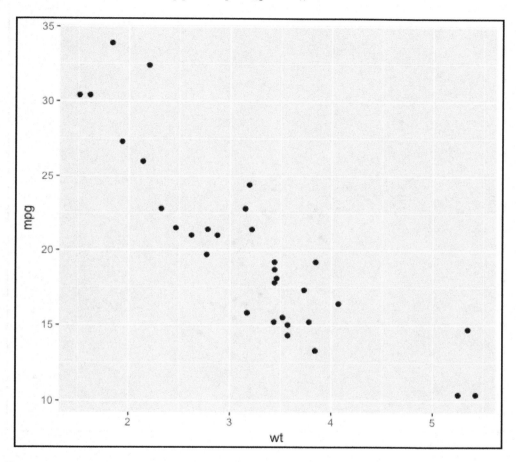

The plot shows a clear relationship between the weight and miles per gallon of the cars, namely as `wt` increases, the `mpg` decreases (we saw this same relationship when we created this plot as a base plot earlier in this chapter).

Though we won't really be able to see much of an effect with this dataset, you can create a scatterplot with a bit of jitter introduced using the following code:

```
ggplot(mtcars, aes(wt, mpg)) + geom_jitter(width = 0.1)
```

You can control exactly how much jitter by inputting `width` = some number into `geom_jitter()`:

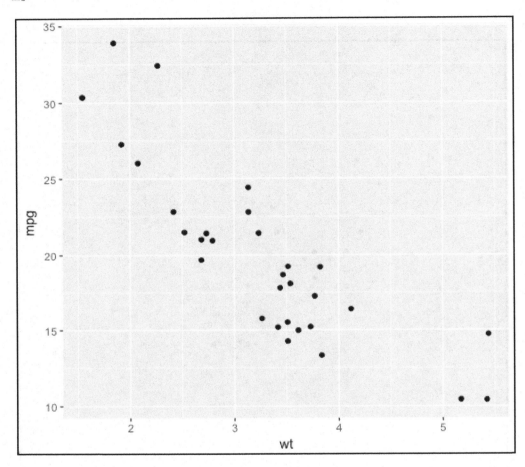

## Creating a Scatterplot of Two Continuous Variables

Let's now create scatterplots using `geom_point()` and `geom_()`.

1. Create a scatterplot of the `bodywt` and `sleep_total` variables from `msleep`:

```
ggplot(msleep, aes(bodywt, sleep_total)) + geom_point()
```

2.  This scatterplot is a great candidate for using `geom_jitter()`, as many of the `sleep_total` observations cluster around the zero bodyweight. We'll use a fairly large width for jitter to really separate these points, because the scale of `bodywt` is in the thousands:

```
ggplot(msleep, aes(bodywt, sleep_total)) + geom_jitter(width = 50)
```

**Output**: The following is the output we get when we execute the code mentioned in *Step 1*:

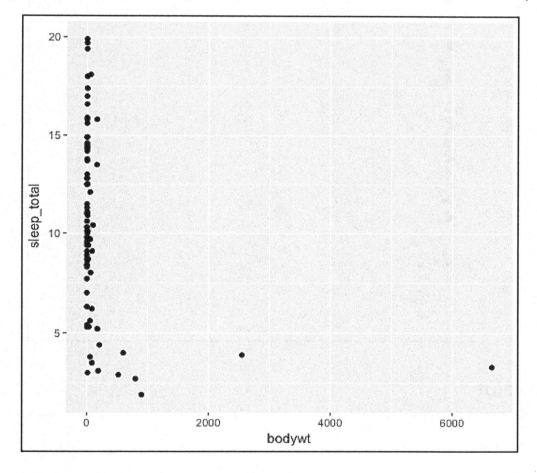

The following is the output we get when we execute the code mentioned in *Step 2*:

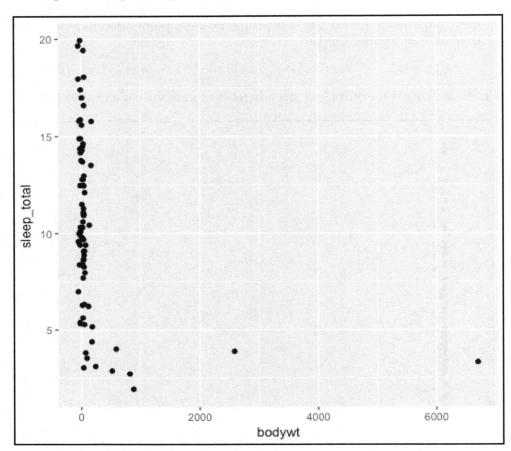

# Boxplot

Boxplots are most appropriate when you want to check the distribution of a continuous *y* variable with some categorical (factor) *x* variable. We cannot create a boxplot of the mpg variable with the cyl variable in mtcars using the following code:

```
ggplot(mtcars, aes(cyl, mpg)) + geom_boxplot()
```

We will get a warning as follows:

```
Warning message: Continuous x aesthetic -- did you forget aes(group=...)?
```

The `cyl` variable is not explicitly declared as a factor variable in the `mtcars` dataset, so ggplot is confused about what the *x* variable is supposed to be. This is similar to when we created base plots with factor variables, though as we saw, `plot()` will still plot a variable not declared as a factor, but it will create a scatterplot instead of the desired histogram. The following code, which transforms `cyl` into a factor variable using `as.factor()`, will fix it and plot the boxplot correctly:

```
ggplot(mtcars, aes(as.factor(cyl), mpg)) + geom_boxplot()
```

Thus, we get the following graph as an output:

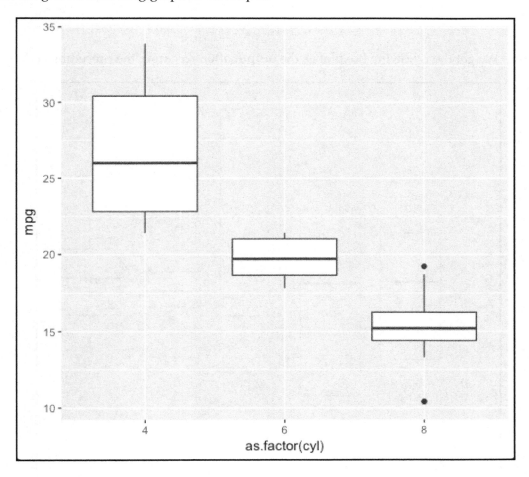

Of course, now the axis label reads `as.factor(cyl)`, because the default axis label is whatever is input as *x*. We'll learn how to fix that in the next subtopic!

## Creating Boxplots using ggplot2

Let us create a boxplot using `geom_boxplot()`.

1.  Create a boxplot of `sleep_total` with `vore`, both variables from the `msleep` dataset using the following code:

 Notice that **omni** seems to have four outliers, represented by the black dots outside of the boxes, which represent the **Interquartile Range (IQR)** of the `sleep_total` of each variable.

```
ggplot(msleep, aes(vore, sleep_total)) + geom_boxplot()
```

**Output**: We get the following boxplot as the output after executing the preceding code:

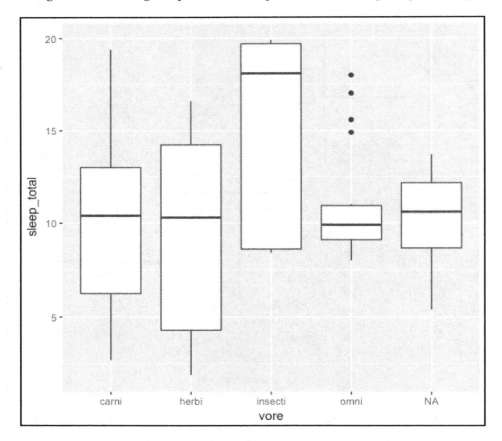

While these four types of plots are far from everything available in ggplot2, everything we've gone over so far in this subtopic should be enough to get started creating basic ggplots. To start, we should get comfortable with building the basics, and then we'll extend them using other calls to `aes()`, plus titles and custom axis labels.

# Activity: Recreating Plots Using ggplot2

**Scenario**

You have been asked to create some ggplots that provide information on the `mtcars` and `iris` datasets for a presentation in your office.

**Prerequisites**

You should have RStudio and R installed on your machine. The ggplot2 package should also be installed.

**Aim**

To construct basic ggplots by recreating some of those shown in the preceding exercises.

**Steps for Completion**

1. Load `ggplot2` using `library(ggplot2)`.

2. Try to recreate all of the following ggplots using the `iris` dataset:
    1. A histogram to plot petal width:

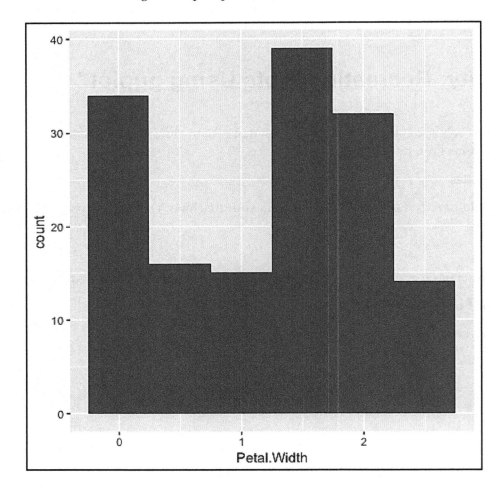

2. A scatterplot to plot petal length and width:

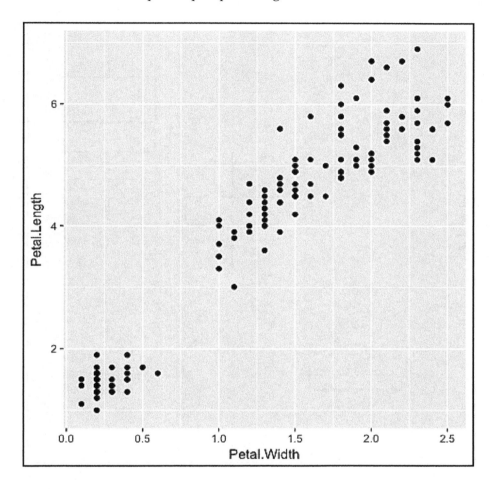

3. Boxplot to plot petal width and the `Species` factor variable:

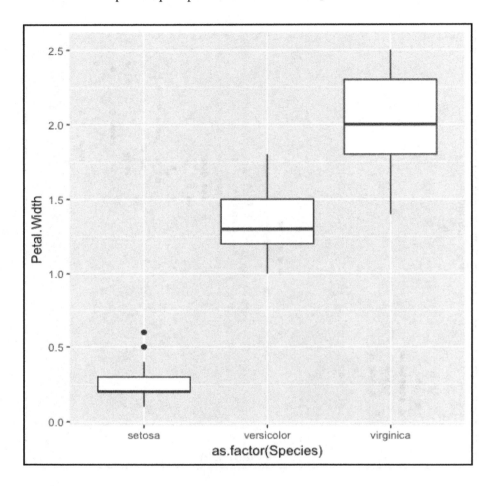

3. Try to recreate the following bar chart ggplot using the `gear` variable of the `mtcars` dataset:

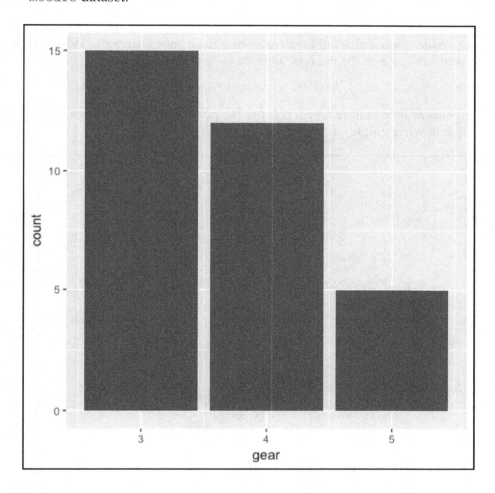

# Digging into aes()

While we have created some basic ggplots, we haven't really dug much into the aesthetics of plots. There are definitely both some global and plot-specific aesthetics that are very important to know when you're building plots.

One key distinction to master is that when you call something inside of `aes()`, the aesthetic is mapped to the value of the variable in the data. Outside of an `aes()` call, the aesthetic is set to a specific value. This is perhaps best understood with an example.

The following code is a bar chart of how many cars have each number of cylinders, where `fill` is the number of gears the car has, all from `mtcars`:

```
ggplot(mtcars, aes(cyl, fill = as.factor(gear))) + geom_bar()
```

A legend appears to let us know which color corresponds to which number of gears, as shown in the following graph:

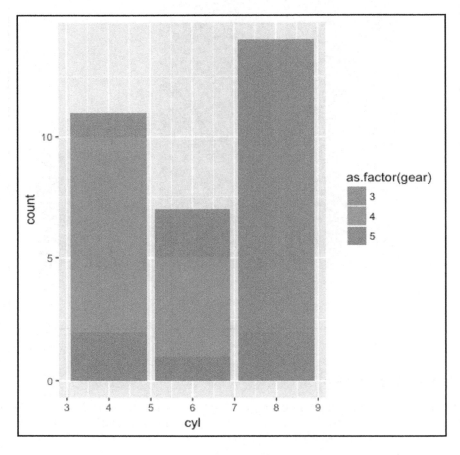

The `fill` is inside of `aes()` and the variable is entered as a factor, both of which are required for this to work.

If, instead, you were looking to make all of the bars light blue, seeing the preceding code, you might be tempted to run the following code:

```
ggplot(mtcars, aes(cyl, fill = "lightblue")) + geom_bar()
```

Or even the following code:

```
ggplot(mtcars, aes(cyl, fill = lightblue)) + geom_bar()
```

However, this code is looking for a thing called lightblue in the dataset, because you entered it inside of aes(). To actually fill the bars light blue, you should use:

```
ggplot(mtcars, aes(cyl)) + geom_bar(fill = "lightblue")
```

This produces the following graph of the bar chart of the count of cars of each cylinder type, but the bars have been colored light blue:

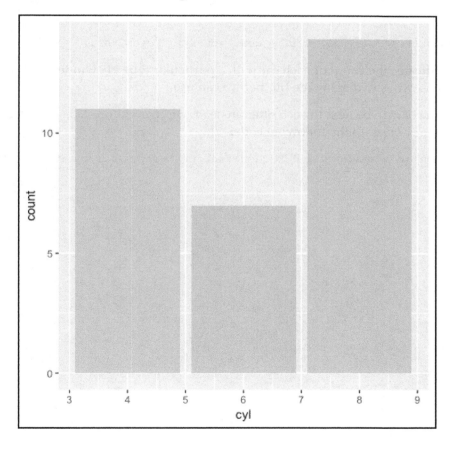

There are some very helpful global and local options that you'll probably need when you're using ggplot2 to create different plots. Let's go through a few of them.

# Bar Chart

To make these charts better, we're going to convert the `cyl` and `gear` variables in `mtcars` to factor variables using the following code:

```
mtcars$cylfactor <- as.factor(mtcars$cyl)
mtcars$gearfactor <- as.factor(mtcars$gear)
```

Use of the factor variables will help the data display properly.

We previously saw how to both automatically change the color of a bar chart (when we made them light blue) and also how to fill a bar chart with another variable. We did this using the following code:

```
ggplot(mtcars, aes(cyl, fill = gearfactor)) + geom_bar()
```

The `fill` indicates the count of each car with a particular type of cylinder and gear. There are a few other ways to display the fill that we can use.

If we want the bars to be next to each other instead, we can add `position = "dodge"` inside `geom_bar()`, with the following code:

```
ggplot(mtcars, aes(cyl, fill = gearfactor)) + geom_bar(position = "dodge")
```

The output will be as shown in the following screenshot:

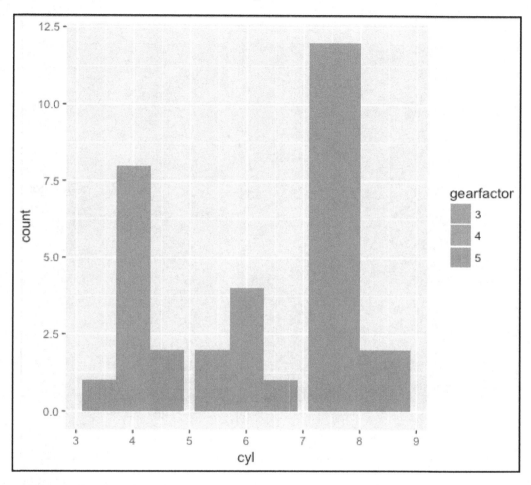

Now, the bars are all next to each other, and it's actually somewhat easier to see that there are no eight-cylinder cars with four gears. ggplot2 also automatically adds a legend to ggplots when you're plotting with colors or shapes.

If we want the bars to reflect percentages instead of representing the count of cars with a certain number of gears and cylinders, we can add position = "fill" inside geom_bar():

```
ggplot(mtcars, aes(cyl, fill = gearfactor)) + geom_bar(position = "fill")
```

The output we get is as follows:

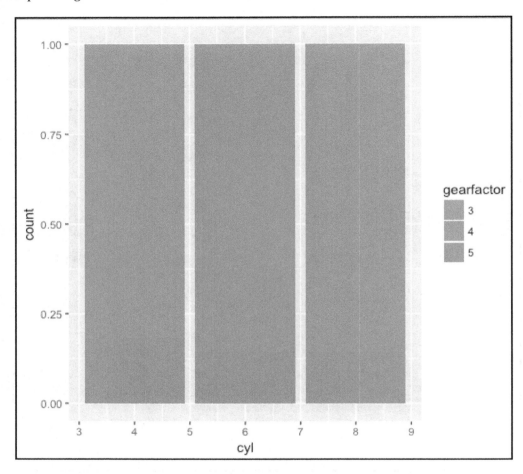

While the *x*-axis still says **count** (we'll be rid of this soon!), it has rescaled from 0 - 1.00, because it represents the percentages instead of counts.

## Using Different Bar Chart Aesthetic Options

Let's now create bar charts using the `dodge` and `fill` bar chart position aesthetic options.

1. If not loaded from the last topic, load the `msleep` dataset using `data("msleep")`.

2. Create a bar chart using the `dodge` position aesthetic of `vore`, filled with the `conservation` variable. (These variables are already declared as factor variables when you load `msleep`.) The code for this is as follows:

```
ggplot(msleep, aes(vore, fill = conservation)) + geom_bar(position = "dodge")
```

3. Create a bar chart with the same variables, this time using the `fill` position aesthetic:

```
ggplot(msleep, aes(vore, fill = conservation)) + geom_bar(position = "fill")
```

**Output**: The following is the output we get when we execute the code mentioned in *Step 1*:

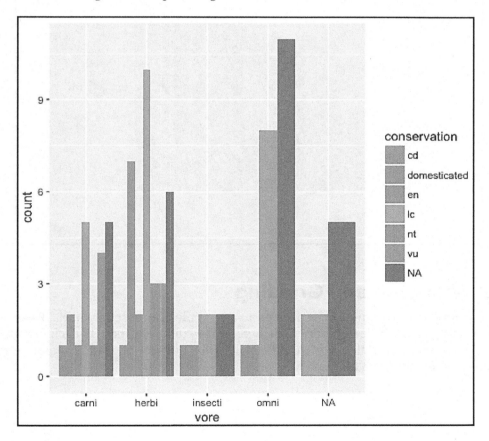

The following is the output we get when we execute the code mentioned in *Step 2*:

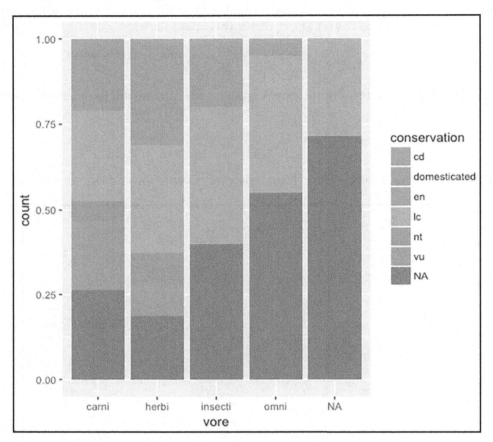

# Facet Wrapping and Gridding

**Facet wrapping** and gridding can be applied to any ggplot, not just bar charts. Facet wrapping will split the base ggplot (which, here, is the count of cars with each number of cylinders) by a second variable, which, here, will be the number of gears, generating three plots. The code for this is as follows:

```
ggplot(mtcars, aes(cylfactor)) + geom_bar() + facet_wrap(~gear)
```

We can see that each of the three numbers of gears (**3**, **4**, **5**) have a bar chart for the count of the number of cars with each of the three types of cylinders (here, `cylfactor`, with values **4**, **6**, **8**). Facet wrapping can be applied to any of the ggplots, though it may sometimes look strange, which can be mitigated with facet gridding.

**Facet gridding** is closely related to facet wrapping but allows for gridding by (`row ~ column`). The following code will generate the same as the preceding facet wrapping code, as gear is in the column place:

```
ggplot(mtcars, aes(cylfactor)) + geom_bar() + facet_wrap(~gear)
```

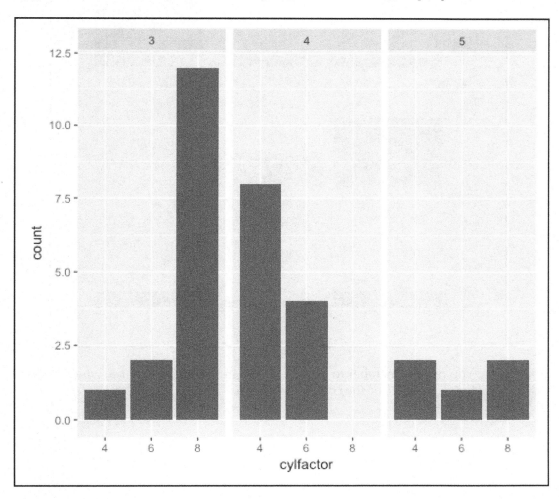

However, if you move gear to the row place, it will grid the plots by row instead of column, as shown in the following code:

```
ggplot(mtcars, aes(cylfactor)) + geom_bar() + facet_grid(gear~)
```

Thus, the output we get will be as follows:

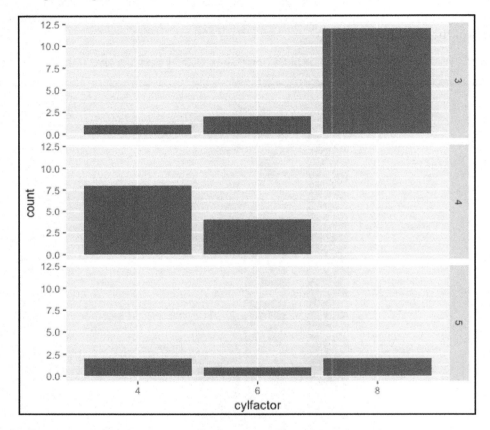

You must remember to put the period in the columns place, which stands for *all columns*, or the code will not run.

## Utilizing Facet Wrapping and Gridding to Visualize Data Effectively

Let's create bar charts using the `facet_wrap()` and `facet_grid()` functions. Follow the steps below:

1. Create a bar chart of `conservation`, facet wrapped by `vore`, both variables from the `msleep` dataset, as shown in the following code:

```
ggplot(msleep, aes(conservation)) + geom_bar() + facet_wrap(~vore)
```

2. Create the same bar chart, but use `facet_grid()` to grid the charts by row instead of column, as shown in the following code:

```
ggplot(msleep, aes(conservation)) + geom_bar() + facet_grid(vore~)
```

**Output**: The following is the output we get when we execute the code in *Step 1*:

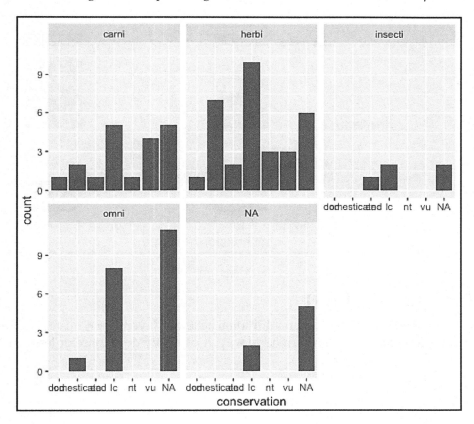

The following is the output we get when we execute the code in *Step 2*:

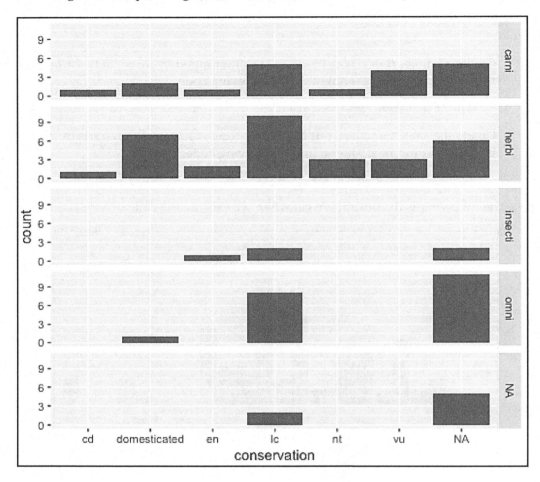

# Boxplot + coord_flip()

One handy feature to know about is an additional aesthetic layer, `coord_flip()`. Given that R functions are named in an informative way, it probably does more or less exactly what you'd think.

Let's return to our boxplot example from mtcars, which shows the distribution of mpg by the number of cylinders. We modify the code and add coord_flip() as follows:

```
ggplot(mtcars, aes(cylfactor, mpg)) + geom_boxplot() + coord_flip()
```

The output we get will be as shown in the following screenshot:

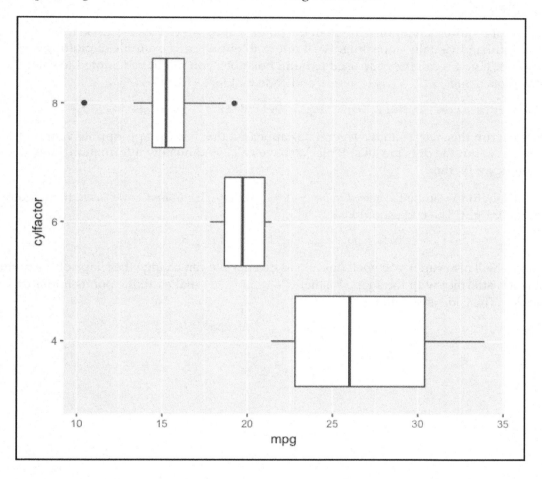

We see that `cylfactor` is now on the *y*-axis and `mpg` is on the *x*-axis, and the boxplots can flip. `coord_flip()` can be implemented on other ggplots as well, but boxplots are a good way to easily see its effect.

# Scatterplot

Scatterplot requires a bit more care than the other graphs we've covered to be truly meaningful and visually appealing. We'll return to our `mtcars` example of plotting `mpg` versus `wt`. If you recall the code used to build boxplots, you might be tempted to color the scatterplots using `fill = cylfactor` and code that looks like this:

```
ggplot(mtcars, aes(wt, mpg, fill = cylfactor)) + geom_point()
```

When we run this, we see that a legend has appeared that has the appropriate values of `cylfactor`, but the dots are all still black, so we've gained no new information. How do you think we fix this?

If you thought to yourself *We need to use* `col = cylfactor` *in that* `aes()` *call*, then you're absolutely right. The code should be:

```
ggplot(mtcars, aes(wt, mpg, col = cylfactor)) + geom_point()
```

The code will also run if you spell out `col` as `color`. We can change the shape of the points inside a scatterplot with the shape aesthetic. `shape = 17` makes all the points into little triangles. The code is as follows:

```
ggplot(mtcars, aes(wt, mpg)) + geom_point(shape = 17)
```

The output we get is as follows:

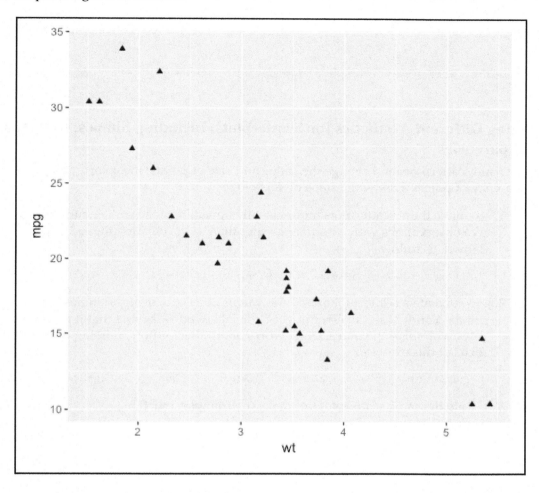

However, these are very tiny. Let's make them bigger with the size options, which we'll also specify inside of geom_point() itself. Here is the code for it:

```
ggplot(mtcars, aes(wt, mpg)) + geom_point(shape = 17, size = 3)
```

Much better! If we had specified color as well, these settings would also apply.

With the bigger size, there's a small amount of overlap with some of the triangles. We can control the transparency using `alpha` = some number between 0 (transparent) and 1 (opaque). Let's start with `alpha = 0.6` and then adjust as needed. Here is the code for that:

```
ggplot(mtcars, aes(wt, mpg)) + geom_point(shape = 17, size = 3, alpha =
0.6)
```

## Utilizing Different Aesthetics for Scatterplots, Including Shapes, Colors, and Transparencies

Let us create scatterplots and change the shape and size of points, the colors, and the transparency of points. Follow the steps given below:

1. To make these scatterplots more visually appealing, load `dplyr` and remove the two observations with a `bodywt` greater than `2000`, creating the `msleep2` dataset, as follows:

   ```
   library(dplyr) msleep2 <- msleep %>% filter(bodywt < 2000)
   ```

2. Now, create a scatterplot of `bodywt` versus `brainwt`, using triangles for the points. You will see an error in your console window saying that it removed rows with missing values. Don't worry about this for now; missing data isn't the focus of this exercise.

   ```
   ggplot(msleep2, aes(brainwt, bodywt)) + geom_point(shape = 17)
   ```

3. Create the same scatterplot but make the triangles much bigger.

   ```
   ggplot(msleep2, aes(brainwt, bodywt)) + geom_point(shape = 17, size
   = 6)
   ```

**Output**: The following is the output we get after executing the code mentioned in *Step 2*:

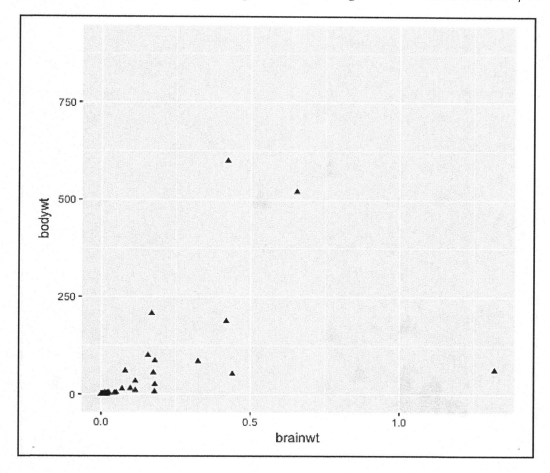

The following is the output we get after executing the code mentioned in *Step 3*:

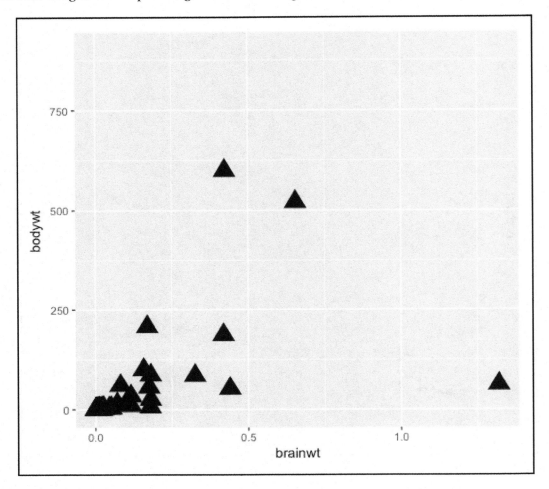

We've covered some global and local aesthetics that are very useful when building ggplots. Let's do a few examples to help master them.

# Activity: Utilizing ggplot2 Aesthetics

## Scenario

You have been asked to create some ggplots that provide information on the `mtcars` and `iris` datasets for a presentation for your colleague, as shown in the following screenshot:

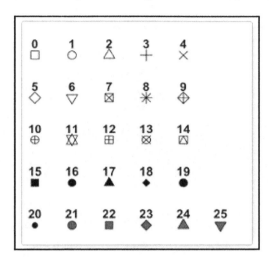

## Aim

To get the students comfortable with using more aesthetic options in their ggplots by having them recreate a few, as shown.

## Prerequisites

Make sure you have R and RStudio installed on your machine. The ggplot2 package should also be installed.

**Steps for Completion**

1. Load `ggplot2` using `library(ggplot2)`.
2. Try to recreate the ggplots shown as follows.
3. The plots use the following datasets:
    - Plots 1 and 2: `mpg`

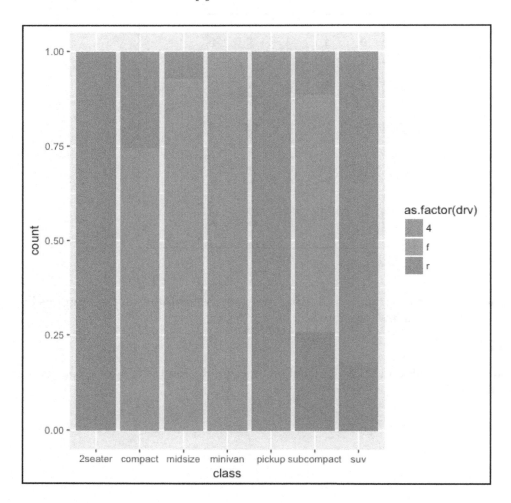

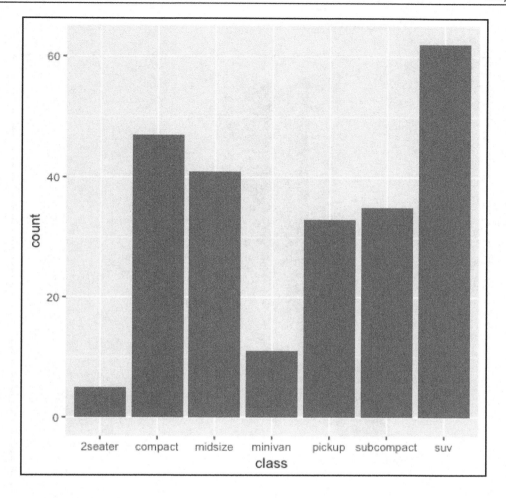

- Plots 3 and 4: `diamonds`

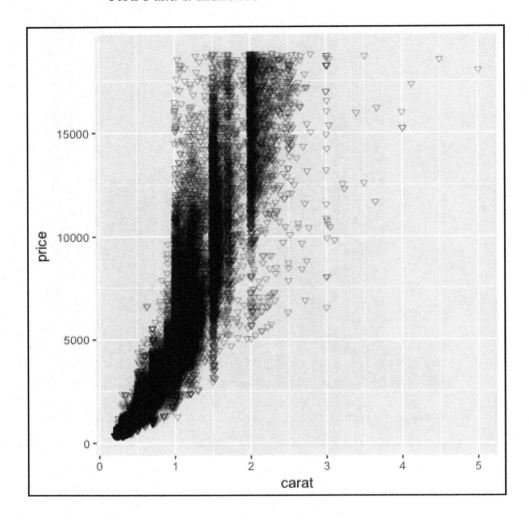

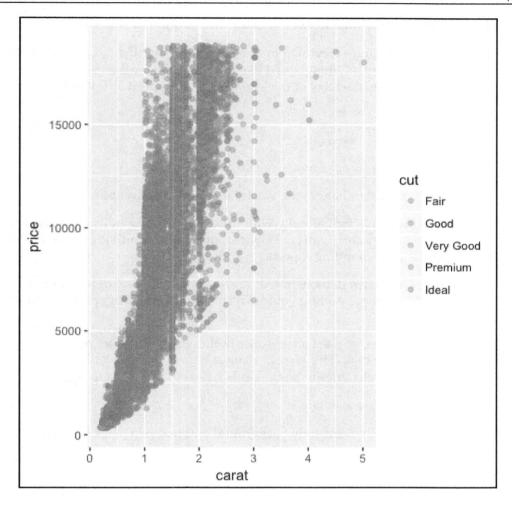

# Extending the Plots with Titles, Axis Labels, and Themes

Thus far, we've learned much of how ggplot2 works by creating a few often-used plots. We have not addressed adding titles, customizing axis labels, or themes. Let's look at the basics of these three things.

Titles and axis labels can be added in two different ways in ggplot2.

If you're interested in changing everything in one go, you can use the labs() function. labs() takes as an argument anything you'd like to change the label of, such as title, subtitle, *x*, *y*, caption, or even the label of the legend. It is often used as follows:

```
mtcars_ggplot + geom_point() +
labs(title = "mpg vs. wt",
     ubtitle = "mtcars dataset",
     x = "weight",
     caption = "decreasing linear trend")
```

This adds a title and a subtitle, changes the *x*-axis label, and adds a caption.

These changes can all be made individually with the corresponding individual functions, such as ggtitle(), xlab(), and ylab(). They can all be added individually as layers to your plot to adjust the corresponding aspects.

Themes make more sense when demonstrated. We'll only cover a few of the built-in ggplot2 themes, but know that building your own custom themes for ggplot2 is entirely possible.

Let's return to an example we've used a few times in this chapter and see how a few different themes change the look. The mtcars dataset with mpg versus wt, colored by cylinder, is a great one. The default theme is theme_gray(), so we'll skip that one.

The other themes available are as follows:

- theme_bw() removes the gray background and makes it black and white. Very straightforward.

- `theme_classic()` removes everything behind the points: there are no secondary axis marks or fill, only blank white space, as shown in the following screenshot:

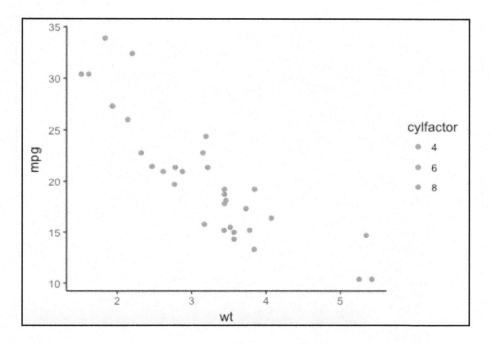

- `theme_dark()` makes everything behind the points a much darker gray. You can see that it also changes the legend to match, as shown in the following screenshot:

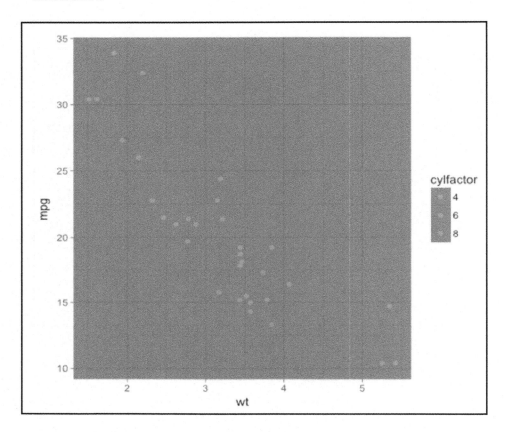

- `theme_minimal()` leaves the axis marks very light gray, but includes no fill. The output is as follows:

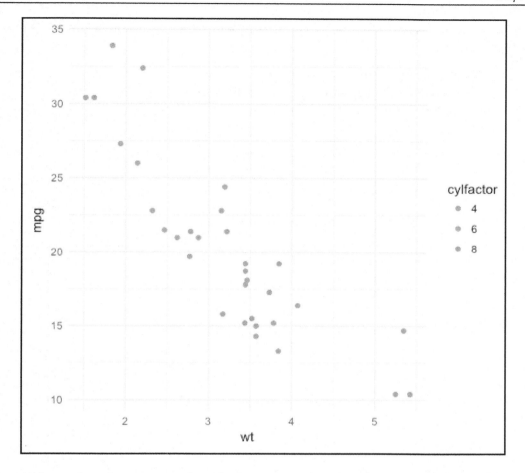

These are just a few theme examples. There are more listed in the documentation that you could experiment with, and you can create your own custom themes once you have more experience with ggplot.

When you're looking to save your ggplots, you have two options. You can use the **export** button above your plot on the **Plots** tab in the viewer, or you can use the `ggsave()` function.

`ggsave("my_mtcars_plot.png")` will save your plot as a PNG with the filename `my_mtcars_plot` in your working directory. If you want to specify another directory, you can do that as well, using `ggsave("images/my_mtcars_plot.png")`, which saves the plot instead in a folder called `images`.

Let us now add titles and axis labels to ggplots by extending the aesthetic options. Follow the steps given below:

1. Load `ggplot2` using `library(ggplot2)`.
2. Try to recreate the ggplots shown as follows. :
   - Execute the following code:

```
library(ggplot2)
ggplot(cars, aes(speed, dist)) + geom_point() +
labs(title = "dist vs. speed",
     subtitle = "cars dataset",
     y = "distance")
```

The output of the preceding code will be as follows:

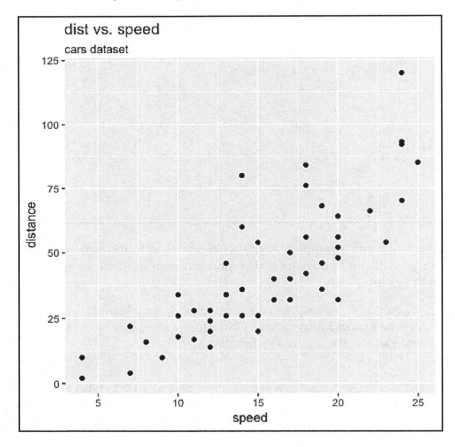

- Execute the following code:

```
ggplot(cars, aes(speed, dist)) + geom_point() +
ggtitle("dist vs. speed",
        subtitle = "cars dataset") +
        ylab("distance")
```

The output of the preceding code will be as follows:

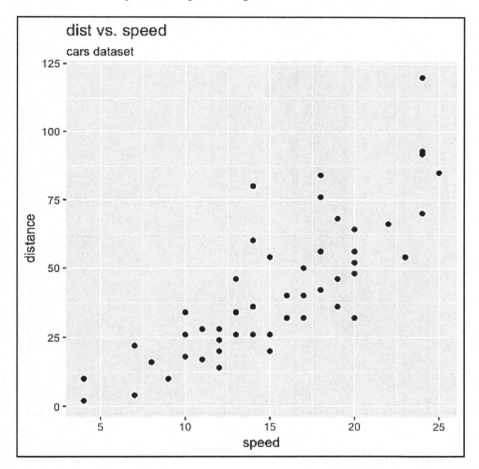

- Execute the following code:

```
ggplot(diamonds, aes(carat, price, col = cut)) +
geom_point(alpha = 0.4) + theme_minimal()
```

The output of the preceding code will be as follows:

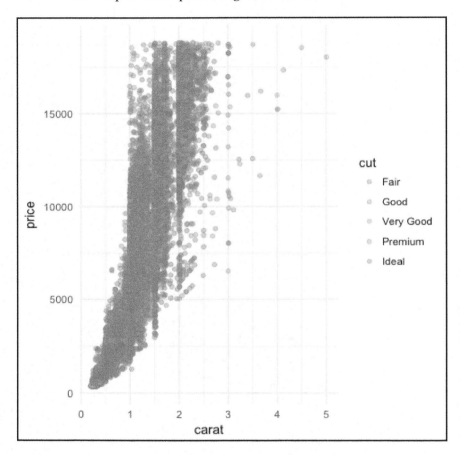

# Interactive Plots

Learning to build interactive plots is not within the scope of this book, but it is likely that you will see (and admire!) them on your data science with R journey, so a few examples are laid out in this topic.

# Plotly

Plotly is an R package designed to allow you to create interactive plots online. It integrates with ggplot2, which we also learned in this chapter, and can be implemented in a number of programming languages as well, including Scala, Python, and Node.js.

We can view a few of these demos on the Plotly website, such as **Dashboards** under **Plotly Fundamentals**. We can see a full dashboard of Plotly charts load, including a plot of the `diamonds` dataset in the upper left, a bar chart next to it, a map of the United States, a heat map, a histogram, and more. Navigate to the Plotly R site and click on the **map demo**:

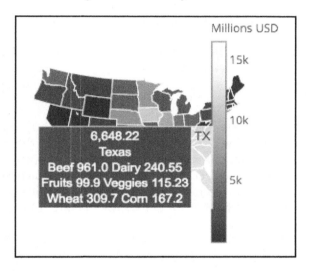

What makes Plotly special is that if we hover over any given part of these examples, we can see values. For example, if we hover over Texas on the map example, we see all of its values in the associated dataset.

Plotly allows for a variety of different charts, such as scatter and line plots, pie charts, box plots, contour plots, heat maps, and beyond. The website gives examples of many, and you can even extend Plotly charts to be interactive or animated.

 Plotly has an entirely online guidebook located at `https://plot.ly/r/`, which demonstrates online and offline uses of Plotly in R.

# Shiny

Shiny is a product built by RStudio that allows you to build interactive web apps straight out of RStudio. They can be used on the web, embedded into R Markdown documents, and like Plotly charts, can be extended with CSS, HTML, and JavaScript.

Shiny allows you to build a number of different kinds of interactive graphics. The **Telephones by Region** example is one that has been built and includes code for you to learn from. If you use the drop-down box to change to different regions, you can see that the number of telephones in the graph changes. Because you can see the code, you can see that for a Shiny app to run, you need two code files: one `server.R` script, and one `ui.R` script, short for user interface, which defines what the graphs in the app will look like.

 Navigate to the RStudio Shiny gallery and see the word cloud example available at the following URL: `https://shiny.rstudio.com/gallery/`.

The **word cloud** example shows a completely different type of Shiny app, which includes a chart we haven't even considered yet. In a word cloud, the size of the word corresponds to how many times it appears in a longer text, with longer words appearing more frequently. There are multiple options we can select in this app, including which Shakespeare text, a minimum frequency, and a maximum number of words. If we adjust all three, we can see that the word cloud changes—we have different words that are different sizes and colors.

While it is not within the scope of this book to build Plotly charts or a Shiny app, once you have the hang of ggplot2 and graphing in R, they are a very fun way to extend your knowledge.

# Exploring Shiny and Plotly

To explore the Shiny and Plotly tools, in your web browser, navigate to the following URLs:

- `https://shiny.rstudio.com/gallery/`
- `https://plot.ly/r/`

Spend some time exploring both sites and find both a Plotly graph and Shiny app that appeal to you.

Can you think of examples of Plotly graphs or Shiny apps you could build in your work? Write your ideas down now so you can learn how to implement them later, after you've finished this book!

# Summary

Graphing in R will be crucial in your data science work, and we have covered most of the basics here. However, graphing is one of those things where, most of the time, there are always going to be different types of graphs you haven't heard of yet and options you haven't yet selected, so it's important to know where to look for assistance and how to keep learning.

We have only covered the basics to get you off the ground in ggplot2 in this book, so you'll definitely need to use Stack Overflow and the ggplot2 official documentation on the `Tidyverse` website to experiment with different graphs and aesthetics. You should look into how to use scales, how to have ggplot2 calculate statistics for you, and the many other different types of plots available.

Let's press forward on to the next topic, where we'll begin to look at some data more closely, doing some cleaning and data management necessary to get us one step closer to modeling and analysis.

# 3
# Data Management

In Chapter 2, *Data Visualization and Graphics*, it was mentioned that data visualization is a key part of EDA. The techniques for data management we'll discuss in this chapter constitute the other important parts of EDA, which you should always do prior to modeling and analysis. In this chapter, we will address what a factor variable is and how to use one, how to summarize your data numerically, how to combine, merge, and split datasets, and how to split and combine strings.

By the end of this chapter, you will be able to:

- Create and reorder factor variables
- Generate pivot tables
- Aggregate data using the base and dplyr packages
- Use various methods to split, apply, and combine data in R
- Split character strings using the stringr package
- Merge and join different datasets using base R and the dplyr methods

# Factor Variables

We discussed variable types in Chapter 1, *Introduction to R*, but did not include factor variables because they're a special type of variable in R that you must often create yourself. In this section, we'll learn what a factor variable is, when to use a factor variable, how to create one, what the levels of a factor are, and how to change the levels.

A factor variable in R is an explicitly declared categorical variable, or one that defines different categories or levels. Some common examples of factor variables include a variable describing sex, month, or one designating low/medium/high.

Recall our discussion of variable classes and types from Chapter 1, *Introduction to R*. A factor variable will always be of class factor, but can be any type: character, numeric, integer, or otherwise. For example, a variable indicating month can have the months as type character ("January", "February", ...) or can be indicated with integers (1, 2, 3, ...).

You can access the class of an object, variable, dataset, or just about anything else in R using this code: class(dataset$variable_name)

You can find out the type of the variable using this code:
typeof(dataset$variable_name)

Let's learn more about what factor variables are and how to use them.

Let's return to the mtcars and iris datasets, both of which we've used previously. (They're very common examples of datasets that are used in R, if you haven't caught on to that yet!) After loading, let's examine each dataset with the method str(), as follows:

```
data("mtcars")
str(mtcars)
data("iris")
str(iris)
```

mtcars has no factor variables specified out of the box, but the Species variable in the iris dataset is explicitly declared to be a factor variable with three levels: setosa, versicolor, and, if we could see it, virginica. We can see all three by using the levels() function, as shown in the following screenshot:

```
> levels(iris$Species)
[1] "setosa"    "versicolor" "virginica"
>
```

Recall that in Chapter 2, *Data Visualization and Graphics*, we examined plotting with factor variables: if you insert a factor into the generic plot() function, you get a bar chart instead of a scatter plot, where the bar chart shows counts of each observation at unique levels of the factor variable.

Since we've discussed what a factor variable is, let's go through some other questions you may have about factors.

**When Should You Use a Factor Variable?**

The cylinder variable in mtcars can be turned into a factor variable because there are only three values the cylinder variable can take. These are four, six, and eight cylinders; this means that this is a *categorical* variable, another word for a factor variable. The cars in this dataset are either four-, six-, or eight-cylinder cars. The mpg variable in the same dataset wouldn't be a good candidate for a factor variable because it isn't categorical and it is the numeric value of the miles per gallon of each car.

Any time you have a character variable that has a set number of categories for that variable, for example, *Months = 12 months, Sex = 2 sexes, 3 levels: Low, Medium,* and *High,* and so on, you can (and should!) transform that variable into a factor variable in R.

**Why Should You Use a Factor Variable?**

Besides the fact that it's helpful to explicitly declare your categorical variables so that these are obvious when you view a summary of a dataset (using str() or dplyr::glimpse()), there are two critical reasons to use factor variables.

Firstly, functions such as `lm()` and `glm()` (among others) that build statistical models in R treat a categorical variable coded with numbers (for example, Months as 1, 2, 3, ...) as a continuous variable if you don't explicitly declare the variable to be a factor variable. This will produce erroneous model estimates and lead to incorrect conclusions.

For example, let's build a linear regression model to examine the relationship between the number of cylinders (`cyl`) and miles per gallon (`mpg`) in cars in the `mtcars` dataset. We'll use `cyl` both as an integer variable and as a factor variable.

We can use `cyl` as an integer variable as follows:

```
summary(lm(mpg ~ cyl, data = mtcars))
```

The output is as follows:

```
Call:
lm(formula = mpg ~ cyl, data = mtcars)

Residuals:
    Min      1Q  Median      3Q     Max
-4.9814 -2.1185  0.2217  1.0717  7.5186

Coefficients:
            Estimate Std. Error t value Pr(>|t|)
(Intercept)  37.8846     2.0738   18.27  < 2e-16 ***
cyl          -2.8758     0.3224   -8.92 6.11e-10 ***
---
Signif. codes:  0 '***' 0.001 '**' 0.01 '*' 0.05 '.' 0.1 ' ' 1

Residual standard error: 3.206 on 30 degrees of freedom
Multiple R-squared:  0.7262,    Adjusted R-squared:  0.7171
F-statistic: 79.56 on 1 and 30 DF,  p-value: 6.113e-10
```

We can use `cyl` as a factor variable as follows:

```
summary(lm(mpg ~ as.factor(cyl), data = mtcars))
```

The output is as follows:

```
Call:
lm(formula = mpg ~ as.factor(cyl), data = mtcars)

Residuals:
    Min      1Q  Median      3Q     Max
-5.2636 -1.8357  0.0286  1.3893  7.2364

Coefficients:
                Estimate Std. Error t value Pr(>|t|)
(Intercept)      26.6636     0.9718  27.437  < 2e-16 ***
as.factor(cyl)6  -6.9208     1.5583  -4.441 0.000119 ***
as.factor(cyl)8 -11.5636     1.2986  -8.905 8.57e-10 ***
---
Signif. codes:  0 '***' 0.001 '**' 0.01 '*' 0.05 '.' 0.1 ' ' 1

Residual standard error: 3.223 on 29 degrees of freedom
Multiple R-squared:  0.7325,    Adjusted R-squared:  0.714
F-statistic:  39.7 on 2 and 29 DF,  p-value: 4.979e-09
```

However, only the output where we've used `cyl` as a factor variable is the correct model output. We want the model to know that that cylinder is a factor and measures the difference in miles per gallon between four and six cylinders and four and eight cylinders; this is the correct way to build the model.

When a variable is categorical and is coded with text, for example, `Months = "January"`, `"February"`, `"March"`, and so on, modeling functions in R automatically treat the variable as categorical, but you should still code it as a factor variable. This is because of the second reason for using factors.

Plots will not render correctly with either base plots or `ggplot2` plots if you do not have your factor variables explicitly declared.

We can rerun the code to plot the `cyl` variable without transforming it into a factor, as follows:

```
plot(mtcars$cyl)
```

We get the scatterplot as an output, as shown in the following screenshot:

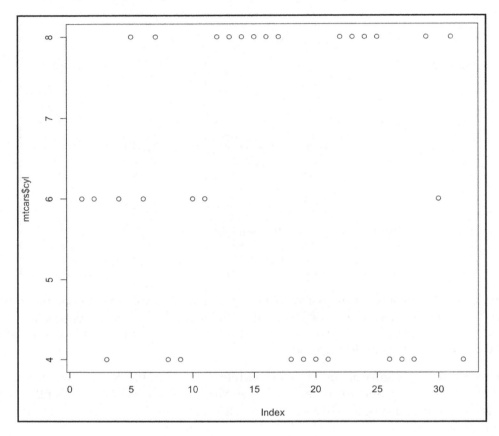

This doesn't really tell us anything about the variable. Similarly, if we try to create a graph using `ggplot2`, for example, by using a boxplot of `mpg` by `cyl` without transforming it into a factor, we'll get a warning:

```
> ggplot(mtcars, aes(cyl, mpg)) + geom_boxplot()
Warning message:
Continuous x aesthetic -- did you forget aes(group=...)?
```

The plot will be only one boxplot, because there's no group variable. Again, this is incorrect and uninformative. Thus, we should change `cyl` into a factor variable using `as.factor()`, as follows:

```
ggplot(mtcars, aes(as.factor(cyl), mpg)) + geom_boxplot()
```

Here is the boxplot we are looking for:

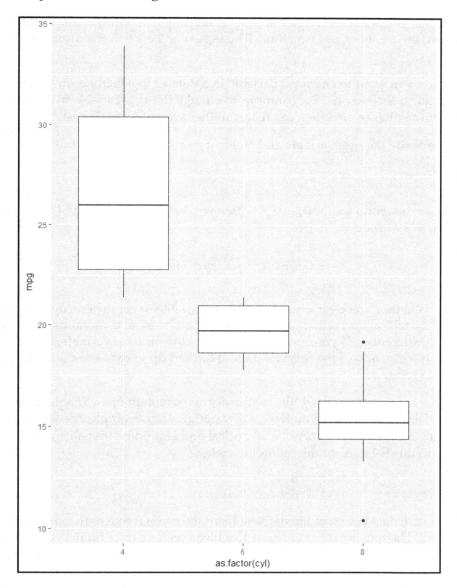

Now that we know when and why to use a factor variable, let's learn how to create one.

### How Should You Create a Factor Variable?

We've seen many times in this chapter and the preceding one that we can create factor variables using the `as.factor()` method. The input can be a variable from a dataset or a vector of values.

Typically, when you want to change a variable in a dataset to a factor, you overwrite the variable or create a second one. For example, to change the `cyl` variable in `mtcars` to a factor, you could either overwrite it or create another variable, as follows:

1.  Overwrite the `cyl` variable and create it as a factor using the following code:

    ```
    mtcars$cyl <- as.factor(mtcars$cyl)
    ```

2.  Create a second variable, `cyl2`, which will be a factor version of the original `cyl` variable as follows:

    ```
    mtcars$cyl2 <- as.factor(mtcars$cyl)
    ```

 Whether you overwrite the original variable or create a second variable is up to you and will depend on the project, storage constraints, and your preferences. If you choose to overwrite the original variable, be sure to have a copy of the original dataset backed up in case something goes wrong!

Often, it will be the case that you'd like to transform more than one variable in your dataset into factor variables. To do this, you have a few options. For example, the variables `cyl`, `am`, and `gear` in the `mtcars` dataset are all categorical and should be transformed to factors. A good way to do this is by using the following code:

```
factors <- c("cyl", "am", "gear")
mtcars[,factors] <- data.frame(apply(mtcars[,factors], 2, as.factor))
```

Here, first, you create a vector of the names of variables you'd like to turn into factors, called `factors`. Then, using `data.frame()`, which creates a data frame, you apply the `as.factor()` function to only the desired columns of the dataset `mtcars`, which are accessed using `mtcars[,factors]`.

The `apply` family of functions provides an efficient way to perform another function on multiple rows or columns of a dataset at once. The input 2 indicates to `apply()` that `as.factor()` should be applied to columns of the dataset `mtcars`. If we had input 1, `as.factor()` would be applied to rows of `mtcars` instead (and likely, this would have returned an error). Applying `as.factor()` by row doesn't really make sense if you think about a row of a dataset. A row of `mtcars` contains all of the information about the car: its `mpg`, `cyl`, `disp`, `hp`, and so on, and only some of these variables are factor/categorical variables. This logic will apply to most datasets you use!

We can check to be sure this worked by using `str()` as follows:

```
str(mtcars)
```

We see that the variables `cyl`, `am`, and `gear` are now all factor variables, as shown in the following screenshot:

```
> str(mtcars)
'data.frame':   32 obs. of  11 variables:
 $ mpg : num  21 21 22.8 21.4 18.7 18.1 14.3 24.4 22.8 19.2 ...
 $ cyl : Factor w/ 3 levels "4","6","8": 2 2 1 2 3 2 3 1 1 2 ...
 $ disp: num  160 160 108 258 360 ...
 $ hp  : num  110 110 93 110 175 105 245 62 95 123 ...
 $ drat: num  3.9 3.9 3.85 3.08 3.15 2.76 3.21 3.69 3.92 3.92 ...
 $ wt  : num  2.62 2.88 2.32 3.21 3.44 ...
 $ qsec: num  16.5 17 18.6 19.4 17 ...
 $ vs  : num  0 0 1 1 0 1 0 1 1 1 ...
 $ am  : num  1 1 1 0 0 0 0 0 0 0 ...
 $ gear: Factor w/ 3 levels "3","4","5": 2 2 2 1 1 1 1 2 2 2 ...
 $ carb: Factor w/ 6 levels "1","2","3","4",..: 4 4 1 1 2 1 4 2 2 4 ...
```

# Creating Factor Variables in a Dataset

Herein, we will create factor variables in a dataset both one at a time and by using a method that converts multiple variables at once. In order to do so, the following steps have to be executed:

1. Load the `datasets` library:

```
library(datasets)
```

2. Load the `midwest` dataset and examine it with `str()`:

```
data(midwest)
str(midwest)
```

3. Convert the `state` variable to a factor by using `as.factor()`:

```
midwest$state <- as.factor(midwest$state)
```

4. Load the `band_instruments` dataset and examine it with `str()`:

```
data(band_instruments)
str(band_instruments)
```

5. Transform both variables in `band_instruments` to factor variables using `apply()`:

```
band_instruments <- data.frame(apply(band_instruments, 2,
as.factor))
```

6. Double-check that *Step 5* worked using `str()`:

```
str(band_instruments)
```

**Output**: The following is the output of the code mentioned in *Step 2*:

```
> str(midwest)
Classes 'tbl_df', 'tbl' and 'data.frame':        437 obs. of  28 variables:
 $ PID           : int  561 562 563 564 565 566 567 568 569 570 ...
 $ county        : chr  "ADAMS" "ALEXANDER" "BOND" "BOONE" ...
 $ state         : chr  "IL" "IL" "IL" "IL" ...
 $ area          : num  0.052 0.014 0.022 0.017 0.018 0.05 0.017 0.027 0.024 0
.058 ...
 $ poptotal      : int  66090 10626 14991 30806 5836 35688 5322 16805 13437 17
3025 ...
 $ popdensity    : num  1271 759 681 1812 324 ...
 $ popwhite      : int  63917 7054 14477 29344 5264 35157 5298 16519 13384 146
506 ...
 $ popblack      : int  1702 3496 429 127 547 50 1 111 16 16559 ...
 $ popamerindian : int  98 19 35 46 14 65 8 30 8 331 ...
 $ popasian      : int  249 48 16 150 5 195 15 61 23 8033 ...
```

The following is the output of the code mentioned in *Step 4*:

```
> str(band_instruments)
Classes 'tbl_df', 'tbl' and 'data.frame':        3 obs. of  2 variables:
 $ name : chr  "John" "Paul" "Keith"
 $ plays: chr  "guitar" "bass" "guitar"
```

The following is the output of the code mentioned in *Step 5*:

```
> str(band_instruments)
'data.frame':      3 obs. of  2 variables:
 $ name : Factor w/ 3 levels "John","Keith",..: 1 3 2
 $ plays: Factor w/ 2 levels "bass","guitar": 2 1 2
```

## How Do You Know if Something is Already a Factor?

You can check if a variable or vector of values is already a factor by using `is.factor()`. It will return `TRUE` or `FALSE` accordingly. Alternatively, you can check the class using `class()` or use `str()` to view either the entire dataset's variable names and types (if you input the dataset name) or just the one variable (if you only input that):

```
> str(iris$Species)
 Factor w/ 3 levels "setosa","versicolor",..: 1 1 1 1 1 1 1 1 1 1 ...
```

## What are the Levels of a Factor, and How Can You Change Them?

The levels of a factor are the particular categories for that variable. They are a special attribute of factor objects in R. You can view them with the `levels()` function, as shown in the following example:

```
levels(iris$Species)
```

It returns the three species of irises indicated in the `Species` variable column, as follows:

```
> levels(iris$Species)
[1] "setosa"     "versicolor" "virginica"
>
```

If we want to change the levels of the factor, we can do so in two ways:

- Using `ifelse()` statements
- Using the `recode()` function

## Using ifelse() Statements

The following code will change the representation of the three species to numbers:

```
iris$Species2 <- ifelse(iris$Species == "setosa", 1,
ifelse(iris$Species == "versicolor", 2, 3))
```

We can verify if it has worked by running the `table()` function as follows (more on this function in the next section!):

```
table(iris$Species)
```

Thus, we will get the following output:

| Setosa | versicolor | verginica |
|--------|------------|-----------|
| 50 | 50 | 50 |

We can also execute the following code to verify whether the representation has changed:

```
table(iris$Species2)
```

Here is the output that we will get:

| 1 | 2 | 3 |
|----|----|----|
| 50 | 50 | 50 |

## Using the recode() Function

The `recode()` function, available in the `dplyr` package, can change the level of the factor by using more readable code, as follows:

```
library(dplyr)
iris$Species3 <- recode(iris$Species,
                        "setosa" = 1,
                        "versicolor" = 2,
                        "virginica" = 3)
```

These are both valid options, and which one you use is up to you.

# Examining and Changing the Levels of Pre-existing Factor Variables

Herein, we will create factor variables in a dataset both one at a time and by using a method that converts multiple variables at once. In order to do so, the following steps have to be executed:

1. Load the `dplyr` library. Use `levels()` to see how many levels of `band_instruments$plays` exist, as follows:

   ```
   levels(band_instruments$plays)
   ```

2. Create a new variable, `plays2`, using `ifelse()` to change the levels bass and guitar to 1 and 2 using the following code:

   ```
   band_instruments$plays2 <- ifelse(band_instruments$plays == "bass",
   1,
   ifelse(band_instruments$plays == "guitar", 2,
   band_instruments$plays))
   ```

3. Use `levels()` to see how many levels of `midwest$state` exist as follows:

   ```
   levels(midwest$state)
   ```

4. Load the `dplyr` library. Create a new variable, `state2`, by using `recode()` to change the levels of the state variable to the states' full names:

```
library(dplyr)
midwest$state2 <- recode(midwest$state,
                         "IL" = "Illinois",
                         "IN" = "Indiana",
                         "MI" = "Michigan",
                         "OH" = "Ohio",
                         "WI" = "Wisconsin")
```

**Output**: The following is the output of the code mentioned in *Step 1*:

```
> levels(band_instruments$plays)
[1] "bass"    "guitar"
```

The following is the output of the code mentioned in *Step 3*:

```
> levels(midwest$state)
[1] "IL" "IN" "MI" "OH" "WI"
```

What about ordered categorical variables?

We've used an example of an ordered categorical variable a few times in this section: a categorical variable that indicates Low/Medium/High is considered ordered. Say we add a variable to the `mtcars` dataset that indicates the car's speed: low, medium, or high. We'll need to set this variable as a factor. When we do so, the code will be as follows:

```
speed <- rep(c("low", "medium", "high"), times = 11)
speed <- speed[-1]
mtcars$speed <- factor(speed, levels = c("low", "medium", "high"), ordered
= TRUE)
```

Now, when we view the class with the `class()` function, we see that it is now as follows:

```
[1] "ordered" "factor"
```

Any time you have a logical order to your factors, it's a good idea to set the `ordered = TRUE` argument.

# Creating an Ordered Factor Variable

Herein, we will create an ordered factor variable in a dataset. In order to do so, the following steps need to be executed:

1. Create a vector called `gas_price` using the following code:

```
gas_price <- rep(c("low", "medium", "high"), times = 146)
gas_price <- gas_price[-1]
```

It will indicate if gas prices in that area are low, medium, or high on average.

2. Add the `gas_price` variable to the `midwest` dataset as follows:

```
midwest$gas_price <- factor(gas_price,
                            levels = c("low", "medium", "high"),
                            ordered = TRUE)
```

3. Verify that the variable has been added to the dataset successfully using `table()` as follows:

```
table(midwest$gas_price)
```

Factor variables are a very important data type in R, since, as we learned previously, plots often won't render correctly unless the variable is explicitly declared to be a factor, and modeling will produce incorrect assumptions if a factor variable is not declared as such.

# Activity: Creating and Manipulating Factor Variables

**Scenario**

You will not be able to avoid using factor variables in your work programming with R, so you set out to learn the best ways to create and manipulate them.

**Aim**

To recognize, create, and manipulate factor variables.

**Prerequisites**

Make sure you have R and RStudio installed on your machine.

**Steps for Completion**

1.  Load the `datasets` library using `library(datasets)`.

2.  Load the `diamonds` dataset:
    *   Examine the dataset with `str()`.
    *   How many factors are present, and what type are they?
    *   Verify with `class()` that they are of the class shown.

3.  Load the `midwest` dataset if it is not already loaded in your environment:
    *   Examine the dataset with `str()`.

    *   Turn all of the character variables into factor variables using the `apply()` method for changing many variables at once.
    *   Check your work with `str()`.

# Summarizing Data

A huge component of data management and cleaning is summarizing your data. It's hard to know what's really inside data just by looking at it. If you're a frequent user of Microsoft Excel, you might be familiar with creating pivot tables to summarize data and get a feel for what's inside your dataset. We won't use pivot tables with R in this book, but it is possible.

There are various R functions and R packages that allow for the creation of different types of tables to examine data. You can also use the `apply` family of functions to generate summaries.

# Data Summarization Tables

If you're familiar with Microsoft Excel, you may have some experience building pivot tables. It's possible to create them in R using the `rpivotTable` package, as shown in the following screenshot:

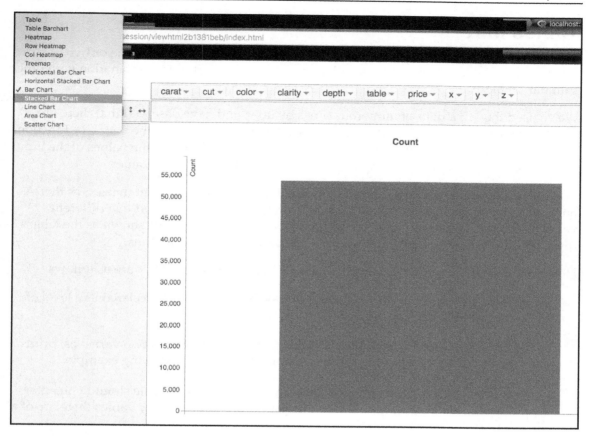

If you install it along with the `htmlwidgets` package, you can create pivot tables with multiple options and look at stats. It's interesting, but you'll also need to know how to manipulate data yourself. The rest of this section will focus on building the various kinds of summaries using tools other than `rpivotTable`.

What kind of data summarization you'll need to use will strongly depend on the goals of your data project. Building a logistic regression model using the classic Titanic passengers' dataset to predict survival? You're going to need to look at sex, passenger class, and age, both on their own and some combination of the three. (We'll clean this dataset later in this chapter.) Writing a report summarizing yearly sales data for the leadership at your company? Look for trends by month, quarter, customer, and product type. You'll need to ask yourself questions about what kinds of data summarizations (and visualizations!) are appropriate and needed. You may not think of them all at once. In fact, EDA is often an iterative process that will happen continuously across data cleaning, modeling, and analysis, and report writing stages of data science.

# Tables in R

Tables in R are very helpful when you want to create a grid of counts of one or two categorical variables. They can be saved as an object for export or in combination with other summary tables.

We've used the `iris` dataset numerous times by now, and have observed that there are 50 of each species of flower in the data. To create a table to verify it, use the `table()` function. If you input a variable of interest to `table()`, R will return a table of the values of the input variable with a count of how many observations have that particular value.

You can also create two-way tables, though we'll need to use a different dataset, as there's only one categorical variable in iris. To create a two-way variable, input two different variables from a dataset into `table()`. The first variable input will be shown as the table's rows, and the second variable input will be shown as the table's columns.

However, there are a few disadvantages of the `table()` function. They are as follows:

- It doesn't show missing variables unless they're explicitly declared as a level of the variable in some way.

- Anything above what a two-way table, that is, a table with two variables, prints is hard to read. You will see an example of this in the following example.

- It prints a long, uninformative table for a continuous variable should you enter one into the function. It won't be helpful to know how many values there are of a variable when it's continuous.

## Creating Different Tables Using the table() Function

Herein, we will use the `table()` function to create three different types of tables in R. In order to do so, the following steps need to be executed:

1. Load the `iris` dataset and create a one-way table of the `Species` variable using the following code:

```
table(iris$Species)
```

2. Load the `diamonds` dataset and create a two-way table of the cut and color variables using the following code:

```
table(diamonds$cut, diamonds$color)
```

3. Create a three-way table of the `cut`, `color`, and `clarity` variables from the diamonds dataset as follows:

```
table(diamonds$cut, diamonds$color, diamonds$clarity)
```

4. Load the `mtcars` dataset if it is not already loaded in your environment. Create a table of the `mpg` variable as follows:

```
table(mtcars$mpg)
```

**Output**: The following is the output we get as we execute the code mentioned in *Step 1*:

| Setosa | versicolor | verginica |
|--------|------------|-----------|
| 50 | 50 | 50 |

The following is the output we get as we execute the code mentioned in *Step 2*:

|           | D    | E    | F    | G    | H    | I    | J   |
|-----------|------|------|------|------|------|------|-----|
| Fair      | 163  | 224  | 312  | 314  | 303  | 175  | 119 |
| Good      | 662  | 933  | 909  | 871  | 702  | 522  | 307 |
| Very Good | 1513 | 2400 | 2164 | 2299 | 1824 | 1204 | 678 |
| Premium   | 1603 | 2337 | 2331 | 2924 | 2360 | 1428 | 808 |
| Ideal     | 2834 | 3903 | 3826 | 4884 | 3115 | 2093 | 896 |

The following is part of the output (it's very long) we get as we execute the code mentioned in *Step 3*:

```
, ,  = I1


              D    E    F    G    H    I    J
Fair          4    9    35   53   52   34   23
Good          8    23   19   19   14   9    4
Very Good     5    22   13   16   12   8    8
Premium       12   30   34   46   46   24   13
Ideal         13   18   42   16   38   17   2

, ,  = SI2


              D    E    F    G    H    I    J
Fair          56   78   89   80   91   45   27
Good          223  202  201  163  158  81   53
Very Good     314  445  343  327  343  200  128
Premium       421  519  523  492  521  312  161
Ideal         356  469  453  486  450  274  110
```

The following is the output we get as we execute the code mentioned in *Step 4*:

```
10.4 13.3 14.3 14.7   15 15.2 15.5 15.8 16.4 17.3 17.8 18.1 18.7 19.2 19.7   21
   2    1    1    1    1    2    1    1    1    1    1    1    1    2    1    2
21.4 21.5 22.8 24.4   26 27.3 30.4 32.4 33.9
   2    1    2    1    1    1    2    1    1
```

For any table above a two-way (or two - variable) table, you're better off turning to methods provided by the `dplyr` package. For example, if we wanted the counts for diamonds by `cut`, `color`, and `clarity`, it's easier to read a table that's been created with `dplyr` methods. `dplyr` will automatically print to the console, but if you'd like to access the tables you create later, you'll need to save the output to your environment. There is a lot of data summarizing that can be accomplished with the `dplyr` package. Let's learn some of the things it can accomplish in the section.

# Using dplyr Methods to Create Data Summary Tables

We will utilize the `dplyr` verbs to create complex data summary tables. In order to do so, the following steps need to be executed:

1. Load the `diamonds` dataset using the following code:

   ```
   data(diamonds)
   ```

2. Group the data by `cut`, `color`, and `clarity`, and find the number of observations at each combination of the three variables, as follows:

   ```
   diamonds %>% group_by(cut, color, clarity) %>% summarise(n())
   ```

3. Find the mean and median price of diamonds by using the `dplyr` functions `group_by()` and `summarise()` as follows:

   ```
   diamonds %>% group_by(cut) %>% summarise(mean = mean(price), median = median(price))
   ```

4. We can also filter out data we're not interested in quickly using `dplyr` methods. Say we don't want any diamonds with color D or J. We can find the mean price by cutting all of the diamonds left in the dataset after removing them:

   ```
   diamonds %>% filter(color != "D" & color != "J") %>% group_by(cut) %>% summarise(mean = mean(price))
   ```

**Output**: Data in the `diamonds` dataset grouped by `cut`, `color`, and `clarity` is as follows:

```
# A tibble: 276 x 4
# Groups: cut, color [?]
   cut    color clarity `n()`
   <ord>  <ord> <ord>   <int>
 1 Fair   D     I1         4
 2 Fair   D     SI2       56
 3 Fair   D     SI1       58
 4 Fair   D     VS2       25
 5 Fair   D     VS1        5
 6 Fair   D     VVS2       9
 7 Fair   D     VVS1       3
 8 Fair   D     IF         3
 9 Fair   E     I1         9
10 Fair   E     SI2       78
# ... with 266 more rows
```

The mean and median price of diamonds is as follows:

```
# A tibble: 5 x 3
        cut      mean median
      <ord>     <dbl>  <dbl>
1      Fair 4358.758 3282.0
2      Good 3928.864 3050.5
3 Very Good 3981.760 2648.0
4   Premium 4584.258 3185.0
5     Ideal 3457.542 1810.0
```

The mean price by `cut` of all of the diamonds left in the dataset after removing them is as follows:

```
# A tibble: 5 x 2
        cut     mean
      <ord>    <dbl>
1      Fair 4311.788
2      Good 3966.567
3 Very Good 3983.078
4   Premium 4597.057
5     Ideal 3515.849
```

Summary tables are incredibly useful and you'll be building a lot of them as you do data science, both with the base `table()` function and with the `dplyr` package. The methods covered here are far from the only way to create data summaries, but are a great start.

# Activity: Creating Data Summarization Tables

### Scenario

You've been asked at work to dig deeper into the diamonds package because your boss is interested in investing company funds in diamonds. Create some explanatory data tables using base R and the `dplyr` methods.

### Aim

To construct basic summary tables by recreating the ones given.

**Prerequisites**

You must have RStudio and R installed on your machine. The datasets package should also be installed.

**Steps for Completion**

1. Load the `dplyr` package.
2. Load the `diamonds` dataset, contained in the `datasets` package. Examine the dataset with `str()`:

```
# A tibble: 8 x 2
  clarity `median(depth)`
  <ord>            <dbl>
1 I1               62.2
2 SI2              61.9
3 SI1              62.0
4 VS2              61.8
5 VS1              61.8
6 VVS2             61.8
7 VVS1             61.7
8 IF               61.7
```

3. Recreate the following summary tables using the `table()` and `dplyr` methods.

The counts of the diamonds' clarity by price are as follows:

```
# A tibble: 56 x 3
# Groups:   color [?]
   color clarity `median(price)`
   <ord> <ord>             <dbl>
 1 D     I1                 3774
 2 D     SI2                3468
 3 D     SI1                1759
 4 D     VS2                1688
 5 D     VS1                1860
 6 D     VVS2               1257
 7 D     VVS1               1427
 8 D     IF                 4632
 9 E     I1                 3296
10 E     SI2                3612
# ... with 46 more rows
```

The counts of the diamonds' clarity by color are as follows:

```
# A tibble: 5 x 2
  color `median(depth)`
  <ord>          <dbl>
1 E               61.8
2 F               61.8
3 G               61.8
4 I               61.9
5 J               62.0
```

# Summarizing Data with the Apply Family

The apply family of functions is an incredibly powerful set of R functions that you should learn early on in your R programming journey. It'll be very helpful to be skilled in summarizing across many variables at once. This is where the apply family of functions comes in.

The apply family is a set of functions that allows you to perform aggregating (using `mean()`, `sum()`, and other summary functions), transforming or sub-setting, and other functions (including custom functions!) across a large range of your dataset. The family of functions includes basic functions such as `apply()`, but also `lapply()`, `sapply()`, `vapply()`, `mapply()`, `rapply()`, and `tapply()`. Mostly, the difference between these different functions is that they return different things when they are called. For example, `lapply()` returns a list and `vapply()` returns a vector. There are a few other differences, but for the purpose of this chapter, they won't be as important.

Let's look at a few examples of how to use the apply family to summarize data. One example of the use of the `apply()` function would be the following:

```
numbers <- rbind(c(1:5), c(2:6)) apply(numbers, 2, mean)
```

The output that we get is the small matrix called numbers, which is represented as follows:

```
> numbers
     [,1] [,2] [,3] [,4] [,5]
[1,]    1    2    3    4    5
[2,]    2    3    4    5    6
```

The parameters passed to `apply()`, in this case, can be explained as follows:

1. The dataframe or matrix to apply a function on (here, `numbers`).
2. The digit indicating if the function is to be applied on columns or rows (here, 2, which in this case means the function will be applied over the columns of the data. If we wanted the mean of every row, we'd use 1 as an input instead.)
3. The function to apply, which in this case is `mean()`.

We used `apply()` here to calculate the mean of every column of the numbers matrix:

```
apply(numbers, 2, mean)
```

Thus, we get the output as follows:

```
[1] 1.5 2.5 3.5 4.5 5.5
```

You can also use multiple functions with `apply()`. Here's an example of that:

```
apply(numbers, 2, function(x) c(median(x), var(x)))
```

The output is as follows:

```
     [,1] [,2] [,3] [,4] [,5]
[1] 1.5 2.5 3.5 4.5 5.5
[2] 0.5 0.5 0.5 0.5 0.5
```

Here, the first two inputs to `apply()` are the same, but we have to write a custom function that takes in a `dataset(x)` and then computes the median and variance of the columns (because we input 2 in the second input to `apply()`) of the dataset.

In the preceding output, the first row is the median of columns and the second is the variance. Not that for the custom function that computes median and variance to work, `median()` and `var()` have to be put inside a vector, which is created with the `c()` function.

The `iris` dataset works very well to demonstrate the power of apply, as it contains only one categorical variable (`Species`) and the rest are continuous. We can find the mean, median, standard deviation, variance, or any numerical summary measure of all four length and width variables quickly with `apply()`. Let's try a few functions out in the next section.

# Using the apply() Function to Create Numeric Data Summaries

Herein, we will utilize the `apply()` function to summarize a dataset. In order to so, the following steps have to be executed:

1. Load the `iris` dataset using the following code:

   ```
   data("iris")
   ```

2. Find the mean of all of the columns of the `iris` dataset except the fifth column (the Species column, which isn't numeric) with the following code:

   ```
   apply(iris[,-c(5)], 2, FUN = mean)
   ```

3. Find the mean and variance of all of the columns of `iris` except the fifth column as follows:

   ```
   apply(iris[,-c(5)], 2, function(x) c(mean(x), var(x)))
   ```

4. Find the mean of all the rows of `iris` as follows:

   ```
   apply(iris[,-c(5)], 1, FUN = mean)
   ```

**Output**: The following is the output we get as we execute the code mentioned in the second step:

```
> apply(iris[,-c(5)], 2, FUN = mean)
Sepal.Length  Sepal.Width Petal.Length  Petal.Width
    5.843333     3.057333     3.758000     1.199333
```

The following is the output we get as we execute the code mentioned in the third step:

```
     Sepal.Length Sepal.Width Petal.Length Petal.Width
[1,]    5.8433333   3.0573333     3.758000   1.1993333
[2,]    0.6856935   0.1899794     3.116278   0.5810063
```

The following is the output we get as we execute the code mentioned in the second step:

```
  [1] 2.550 2.375 2.350 2.350 2.550 2.850 2.425 2.525 2.225 2.400 2.700 2.500
 [13] 2.325 2.125 2.800 3.000 2.750 2.575 2.875 2.675 2.675 2.675 2.350 2.650
 [25] 2.575 2.450 2.600 2.600 2.550 2.425 2.425 2.675 2.725 2.825 2.425 2.400
 [37] 2.625 2.500 2.225 2.550 2.525 2.100 2.275 2.675 2.800 2.375 2.675 2.350
 [49] 2.675 2.475 4.075 3.900 4.100 3.275 3.850 3.575 3.975 2.900 3.850 3.300
 [61] 2.875 3.650 3.300 3.775 3.350 3.900 3.650 3.400 3.600 3.275 3.925 3.550
 [73] 3.800 3.700 3.725 3.850 3.950 4.100 3.725 3.200 3.200 3.150 3.400 3.850
 [85] 3.600 3.875 4.000 3.575 3.500 3.325 3.425 3.775 3.400 2.900 3.450 3.525
 [97] 3.525 3.675 2.925 3.475 4.525 3.875 4.525 4.150 4.375 4.825 3.400 4.575
[109] 4.200 4.850 4.200 4.075 4.350 3.800 4.025 4.300 4.200 5.100 4.875 3.675
[121] 4.525 3.825 4.800 3.925 4.450 4.550 3.900 3.950 4.225 4.400 4.550 5.025
[133] 4.250 3.925 3.925 4.775 4.425 4.200 3.900 4.375 4.450 4.350 3.875 4.550
[145] 4.550 4.300 3.925 4.175 4.325 3.950
```

# Activity: Implementing Data Summary

### Scenario

You need to teach a coworker how to use apply functions. You write them a reproducible example using the mtcars dataset.

### Aim

To summarize the variables in the mtcars data set using apply().

### Prerequisites

Make sure you have R and RStudio installed on your machine. The datasets package should be installed.

### Steps for Completion

1. Load the mtcars dataset, if it currently isn't loaded in your R environment, and examine the data with str().
2. Use apply() to summarize all of the variables in mtcars that are not categorical. Find the mean and variance of each.

# Splitting, Combining, Merging, and Joining Datasets

Any time you're working with data, which R is designed for, you're likely to encounter a number of situations where you'll need to either split up datasets, combine them, or merge/join them. Occasionally in your work, you may be handed data that is already in one dataset that you'll use throughout the analysis. However, it's more likely that you'll need to do a decent amount of splitting, combining, and merging/joining over the course of any given project.

## Splitting and Combining Data and Datasets

Splitting and unsplitting data is provided for in the base package of R with functions named `split()` and `unsplit()`. Combining data is usually done using the base functions `rbind()` and `cbind()`, which combine by row and column, respectively. Let's look at how to split, unsplit, and combine data in R.

## Splitting and Unsplitting Data with Base R and the dplyr Methods

Splitting data can be accomplished using base R with the `split()` function. Its simplest use would be to input a dataset you'd like to be split followed by a factor variable to split that dataset `by`. `unsplit()` works in a very similar fashion.

`dplyr` also has functions that facilitate splitting data, which can be rejoined with combination methods we will cover in more detail very soon in this section. Often, these alternative methods will require less code.

Let's explore both of these possibilities in the next section.

## Splitting Datasets into Lists and Then Back Again

Herein, we will utilize the `split()` and `unsplit()` functions to separate and recreate datasets, and then use `filter()` from `dplyr` to supplement knowledge of how to split data.

In order to do so, the following steps have to be executed:

1. Load the `iris` dataset if it is not currently loaded using the following code:

   ```
   data(iris)
   ```

2. Split the `iris` dataset by species. This creates three lists of dataframes, each of which will only contain the information about one species of iris represented in the data. Verify that `iris_species` is a list by checking its type and check the class of `iris_species[[1]]`. This can be done with the help of the following code:

   ```
   iris_species <- split(iris, iris$Species)
   typeof(iris_species)
   class(iris_species[[1]])
   ```

3. Print the head of the second dataframe, which contains all the versicolor iris data using the following code:

   ```
   head(iris_species[[2]])
   ```

4. Assign each dataframe into its own separate data object. Name the dataframes after the species of iris contained inside, as follows:

   ```
   iris_setosa <- iris_species[[1]]
   iris_versicolor <- iris_species[[2]]
   iris_virginica <- iris_species[[3]]
   ```

5. Use `unsplit()` to recombine `iris_species` into `iris_back`, which should be identical to the original `iris` dataset. Verify that they are identical using `all_equal()` from `dplyr`, which compares every aspect of the two dataframes. It can be done using the following code:

   ```
   iris_back <- unsplit(iris_species, iris$Species)
   library(dplyr)
   all_equal(iris, iris_back)
   ```

6. Since `dplyr` is now loaded, recreate the three different `iris` datasets using `filter()` on `iris` to retain only one species of iris at a time. This method involves less code than using `split()` to create a list of dataframes by allowing you to create each dataframe directly:

   ```
   iris_setosa_2 <- iris %>% filter(Species == "setosa")
   iris_versicolor_2 <- iris %>% filter(Species == "versicolor")
   iris_virginica_2 <- iris %>% filter(Species == "virginica")
   ```

7. Rejoin the three new iris dataframes by using `rbind.as.data.frame()`, and verify that it's the same as iris by using `all_equal()`:

```
iris_back_2 <- rbind.data.frame(iris_setosa_2, iris_versicolor_2,
iris_virginica_2)
all_equal(iris, iris_back_2)
```

**Output**: The following is the output we get as we execute the code from the second step:

```
[1]   "list"

[1]   "dat.frame"
```

The following is the output we get as we execute the code from the third step:

|    | Sepal.Length | Sepal.Width | Petal.Length | Petal.Width | Species |
|----|--------------|-------------|--------------|-------------|-----------|
| 51 | 7.0 | 3.2 | 4.7 | 1.4 | versicolor |
| 52 | 6.4 | 3.2 | 4.5 | 1.5 | versicolor |
| 53 | 6.9 | 3.1 | 4.9 | 1.5 | versicolor |
| 54 | 5.5 | 2.3 | 4.0 | 1.3 | versicolor |
| 55 | 6.5 | 2.8 | 4.6 | 1.5 | versicolor |
| 56 | 5.7 | 2.8 | 4.5 | 1.3 | versicolor |

The following is the output we get as we execute the code mentioned in the sixth step:

```
[1]   TRUE
```

The following is the output we get as we execute the code mentioned in the seventh step:

```
[1]   TRUE
```

# Combining Data

`rbind()` and `cbind()` are two major combining functions you can use in R. We just used the `rbind.data.frame()` function to recombine the iris datasets, and you may recall that we covered both of these functions in *Chapter 1, Introduction to R*, in detail. As a reminder, they combine data by row and column, respectively. As a quick review, let's combine some data in the next section.

# Combining Data with rbind()

Herein, we will demonstrate the power of `rbind()` for combining data. In order to do so, the following steps need to be executed:

1. Install and load the `ggplot2` package, as it contains the `midwest` dataset:

   ```
   install.packages("ggplot2") library(ggplot2)
   ```

2. Load the `midwest` data and examine its contents with `str()`:

   ```
   data("midwest") str(midwest)
   ```

3. We'll first need to split the data in order to combine it. Let's split it evenly, in half, to create `midwest_1` and `midwest_2`. We can calculate directly in our subsetting method to get half of the number of rows of `midwest` in each dataset:

   ```
   midwest1 <- midwest[1:round(nrow(midwest)/2),]
   midwest2 <-
   midwest[(round(nrow(midwest)/2)+1):nrow(midwest),]
   ```

4. Recombine `midwest` into `midwest_back` using `rbind()` to combine by rows (because we split in half by rows!):

   ```
   midwest_back <- rbind(midwest1, midwest2)
   ```

5. Check to see if `midwest_back` is the same as `midwest` using `all_equal()`, like we did previously:

   ```
   all_equal(midwest, midwest_back)
   ```

**Output**: The following is the output we get as we execute the code mentioned in *Step 2*:

```
Classes 'tbl_df', 'tbl' and 'data.frame':      437 obs. of  28 variables:
 $ PID                 : int  561 562 563 564 565 566 567 568 569 570 ...
 $ county              : chr  "ADAMS" "ALEXANDER" "BOND" "BOONE" ...
 $ state               : chr  "IL" "IL" "IL" "IL" ...
 $ area                : num  0.052 0.014 0.022 0.017 0.018 0.05 0.017 0.027 0.024 0.058 ...
 $ poptotal            : int  66090 10626 14991 30806 5836 35688 5322 16805 13437 173025 ...
 $ popdensity          : num  1271 759 681 1812 324 ...
 $ popwhite            : int  63917 7054 14477 29344 5264 35157 5298 16519 13384 146506 ...
 $ popblack            : int  1702 3496 429 127 547 50 1 111 16 16559 ...
 $ popamerindian       : int  98 19 35 46 14 65 8 30 8 331 ...
 $ popasian            : int  249 48 16 150 5 195 15 61 23 8033 ...
 $ popother            : int  124 9 34 1139 6 221 0 84 6 1596 ...
 $ percwhite           : num  96.7 66.4 96.6 95.3 90.2 ...
 $ percblack           : num  2.575 32.9 2.862 0.412 9.373 ...
 $ percamerindan       : num  0.148 0.179 0.233 0.149 0.24 ...
 $ percasian           : num  0.3768 0.4517 0.1067 0.4869 0.0857 ...
 $ percother           : num  0.1876 0.0847 0.2268 3.6973 0.1028 ...
 $ popadults           : int  43298 6724 9669 19272 3979 23444 3583 11323 8825 95971 ...
 $ perchsd             : num  75.1 59.7 69.3 75.5 68.9 ...
 $ percollege          : num  19.6 11.2 17 17.3 14.5 ...
 $ percprof            : num  4.36 2.87 4.49 4.2 3.37 ...
 $ poppovertyknown     : int  63628 10529 14235 30337 4815 35107 5241 16455 13081 154934 ...
 $ percpovertyknown    : num  96.3 99.1 95 98.5 82.5 ...
 $ percbelowpoverty    : num  13.15 32.24 12.07 7.21 13.52 ...
 $ percchildbelowpovert: num  18 45.8 14 11.2 13 ...
 $ percadultpoverty    : num  11.01 27.39 10.85 5.54 11.14 ...
 $ percelderlypoverty  : num  12.44 25.23 12.7 6.22 19.2 ...
 $ inmetro             : int  0 0 0 1 0 0 0 0 0 1 ...
 $ category            : chr  "AAR" "LHR" "AAR" "ALU" ...
```

The following is the output we get as we execute the code mentioned in *Step 5*:

```
[1]   TRUE
```

If you use rbind() to combine data, you'll need the same amount of columns in the data you are combining. If you use cbind(), you'll need to have the same number of rows in the data you're combining.

One nice feature of the functions rbind() and cbind() is that they can combine more than two items to create a new dataset.

# Combining Matrices of Objects into Dataframes

Herein, we will use rbind() and cbind(), plus their associated data.frame methods, to combine multiple R objects into dataframes. In order to do so, the following steps have to be executed:

1. Create one, two, three, and four, which are all vectors of sequential numbers:

   ```
   one <- 1:15
   two <- 16:30
   three <- 31:45
   four <- 46:60
   ```

2. Create all1 and all2 from one, two, three, and four. all1 should be combined by rows, while all2 should be combined by columns:

   ```
   all1 <- rbind(one, two, three, four)
   all2 <- cbind(one, two, three, four)
   ```

3. Check the class of all1:

   ```
   class(all1)
   ```

4. Recombine one, two, three, and four into data.frames and look at the class of all3:

   ```
   all3 <- rbind.data.frame(one, two, three, four)
   all4 <- cbind.data.frame(one, two, three, four)
   class(all3)
   ```

**Output**: The following is the output we get as we execute the code class(all1):

```
[1]    "Matrix"
```

The following is the output we get as we execute the code mentioned in the last *Step 4*:

```
[1]    "data.frame"
```

## Splitting Strings

One other useful type of splitting is the ability to split strings. While this isn't a data splitting and unsplitting method, it will often be useful to do the following to manipulate variables in a dataset. The most efficient way to accomplish string splitting in R is to use the stringr package, which contains a variety of functions that make working with strings far simpler than alternative methods in base, which include subset() and gsub(). We won't cover these methods here, however the stringr methods are highly recommended, are far more versatile, and often don't require you to write complicated regex patterns for matching.

 A *regex*, or regular expression, is a search method used to match certain things in text. Look up regex on the search engine of your choice and read more about them if you're interested.

From the stringr package, the str_split() function in particular is useful. Let's dive in and look at some different ways it can be used.

## Using stringr Package to Manipulate a Vector of Names

Herein, we will utilize the str_split() function to learn how to split character strings in R. In order to do so, the following steps need to be executed:

1.  Install and then load the stringr package:

    ```
    install.packages("stringr") library(stringr)
    ```

2. Create the names vector, a list of various names, and check its length to see how many names it contains:

```
names <- c("Danelle Lewison", "Reyna Wieczorek", "Jaques Sola",
"Marcus Huling", "Elvis Driver", "Chandra Picone", "Alejandro
Caffey", "Shawnna Lomato", "Masako Hice", "Wally Ota", "Phillip
Batten", "Denae Rizzuto", "Joseph Merlos", "Maurice Debelak",
"Carina Gunning", "Tama Moody") length(names)
```

3. Use `str_split()` to separate each name into first name and surname and save it as an object called `names_split`. `str_split()` takes two arguments: the vector (or character string) you plan to split, and a pattern to split on:

```
names_split <- str_split(names, pattern = " ")
```

4. Examine the first split name in `names_split`. Then, look at the first name. Remember to use list indexing, as `names_split` is a list of the split first names and surnames:

```
names_split[[1]]
names_split[[1]][1]
```

5. Split create `names_split_a`, which splits names at any *a*s in each name. You only have to change one of the inputs to `str_split()` that you used previously:

```
names_split_a <- str_split(names, pattern = "a")
```

6. Examine the first split name and the second half of the first split name in `names_split_a` once more. How has it been split differently?

```
names_split_a[[1]] names_split_a[[1]][2]
```

7. Now, examine the fifth split name from `names_split_a`. What happened with this name that has no a in it?

```
names_split_a[[5]]
```

**Output**: The following is the output we get upon executing the code mentioned in *Step 2*:

```
[1]    16
```

The following is the output we get upon executing the code mentioned in *Step 4*:

```
[1] "Danelle" "lewison"
[1] "Danelle"
```

The following is the output we get upon executing the code mentioned in *Step 6*:

```
[1] "Elvis Driver"
```

Text cleaning is a big part of data cleaning, and will often require even more work than string splitting. You should check out the many functions included in the stringr package in any instance in the future where you're asked to work with text data in R.

Combining strings is so straightforward; you can use base R methods to do so: use paste() to combine strings with a space in between the items you're combining, and paste0() to combine strings without a space.

## Combining Strings Using Base R Methods

Herein, we will use paste() and paste0() with character objects, character strings, and integers. In order to do so, the following steps have to be executed:

1. Create variables a, b, and c, which contain character strings:

   ```
   a <- "R"
   b <- "is"
   c <- "fun"
   ```

2. Use paste() to combine a, b, and c with an exclamation mark:

   ```
   paste(a, b, c, "!")
   ```

3. Use paste0() to do the same, but without spaces between a, b, c, and the exclamation mark:

   ```
   paste0(a, b, c, "!")
   ```

4. Use paste() to create the string "R is fun x 10" with the objects you've created:

   ```
   paste(a, b, c, "x", 10)
   ```

**Output**: The following is the output we get upon executing the code mentioned in *Step 2*:

```
[1] "R is fun !"
```

The following is the output we get upon executing the code mentioned in *Step 3*:

```
[1] "Risfun!"
```

The following is the output we get upon executing the code mentioned in *Step 4*:

```
[1] "R is fun x 10"
```

Splitting and combining both data and character strings are important skills for programming with R. Often, they'll be used as part of a workflow known as split-apply-combine, where you split a dataset as needed, apply various summaries and other functions to it, and then recombine the summarized data, now transformed and exactly how you need it.

# Activity: Demonstrating Splitting and Combining Data

**Scenario**

You need to split the mtcars dataset by cylinder type for a project. You also want to recombine the datasets to understand the power of combining data in R.

**Aim**

To get comfortable with both splitting and combining datasets.

**Prerequisites**

Make sure you have R and RStudio installed on your machine.

## Steps for completion

1. Load the `mtcars` dataset.
2. Split the data by the `cyl` variable.
3. Create a dataset for each level of `cyl`.
4. Recreate `mtcars` by unsplitting the split version of the data.
5. Create the following two datasets by combining the data:

   `letters1` dataset:

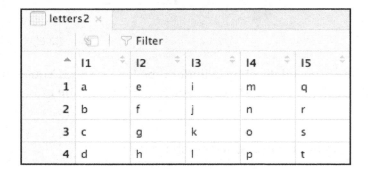

| | c..a...e....i....m....q.. | c..b....f....j....n....r.. | c..c....g....k....o....s.. | c..d....h....l....p....t.. |
|---|---|---|---|---|
| 1 | a | b | c | d |
| 2 | e | f | g | h |
| 3 | i | j | k | l |
| 4 | m | n | o | p |
| 5 | q | r | s | t |

   `letters2` dataset:

| | l1 | l2 | l3 | l4 | l5 |
|---|---|---|---|---|---|
| 1 | a | e | i | m | q |
| 2 | b | f | j | n | r |
| 3 | c | g | k | o | s |
| 4 | d | h | l | p | t |

# Merging and Joining Data

Many of the examples we see, both in this book and in many spaces where we learn to program in R or other languages, include complete datasets. The datasets we're using for much of this book are built-in and don't need to be merged with any other data. This is very rarely the case when you're actually doing data analysis. One crucial skill in data science especially is the ability to merge and join data, by a common key, from occasionally disparate sources. Base R allows for merging datasets with the merge function. Inside of it, you can specify the type of merge, which you might be familiar with if you've ever used SQL to merge data. Joins are implemented in R inside the dplyr package. Say we have two datasets, x and y, and we want to join them using a variable ID, which perhaps identifies unique subjects in datasets x and y. Here's a summary of the types of merges and joins you'll use most of the time:

| Type of Join | Rows | Columns | merge() argument |
|---|---|---|---|
| Inner | All from *x* where there are matching values of ID in *y*. If multiple matches of ID exist, there will be multiple rows of that ID. | All from *x* and *y* | Default–no additional argument needed |
| Semi | All from *x* where there are matching values of ID in *y*. Never returns multiple matches. | Only those from *x* | N/A |
| Left | All from *x*. If multiple matches of ID exist, there will be multiple rows of that ID. | All from *x* and *y* | all.x = TRUE |
| Right | All from *y*. If multiple matches of ID exist, there will be multiple rows of that ID. | All from *x* and *y* | all.y = TRUE |
| Full | All from *x* and *y*. If no matching values on ID from *x* and *y*, there will be an NA for the missing. | All from *x* and *y* | all = TRUE |

Let's look at how to perform merges and joins in R with an example. Let's return to the students dataset that we used in *Chapter 1, Introduction to R*, with the addition of an ID variable, a unique number assigned to each individual student. We'll also use a second dataset, `students2`, which gives more information about these students, including their gender, grade, and what sport they play. These two datasets have an ID variable in common, so we'll be able to merge and join on this variable.

# Demonstrating Merges and Joins in R

Herein, we will use the base R `merge()` function and the `dplyr` join functions to work out how to merge and join data in R, comparing and contrasting the two functions throughout.

In order to do so, the following steps need to be executed:

1. Install and load the `readr` package, which contains functions that read in data much faster than the `baseR` data read functions:

   ```
   install.packages("readr") library(readr)
   ```

2. Download the `students` and `students2` datasets from the GitHub repository:

   ```
   students <- read_csv("https://raw.githubusercontent.com/
   TrainingByPackt/R-Programming-
   Fundamentals/master/lesson3/students.csv")
   students2 <- read_csv("https://raw.githubusercontent.com/
   TrainingByPackt/R-Programming-
   Fundamentals/master/lesson3/students2.csv")
   ```

3. Examine both datasets using `str()`. Verify that they each has an ID variable, and take note that students has information about 20 students (20 observations), while `students2` has information on five additional students (25 observations):

   ```
   str(students) str(students2)
   ```

4. Create `students_combined` by merging the two datasets by ID. Check the dimensions of students combined to see how many students' information is retained on this inner join. There should only be 20 matches on ID between the two datasets on this default inner join:

   ```
   students_combined <- merge(students, students2, by = "ID")
   dim(students_combined)
   ```

5.  Create `students_combined2`, this time performing a right join using `merge()`, which should retain all of the possible students' information. Check the dimensions to see how much of students' information is in the combined dataset. Does it match up with your expectations?

```
students_combined2 <- merge(students, students2, by = "ID", all.y =
TRUE) dim(students_combined2)
```

You'll see the following output:

| | ID | Height_inches | Weight_lbs | EyeColor | HairColor | USMensShoeSize | Gender | Grade | Sport |
|---|---|---|---|---|---|---|---|---|---|
| 1 | 1 | 65 | 120 | Blue | Brown | 9 | F | 9 | Basketball |
| 2 | 2 | 55 | 135 | Brown | Blond | 5 | F | 9 | Track |
| 3 | 3 | 60 | 166 | Hazel | Black | 6 | M | 12 | Tennis |
| 4 | 4 | 61 | 154 | Brown | Brown | 7 | M | 11 | None |
| 5 | 5 | 62 | 189 | Green | Blond | 8 | M | 10 | Tennis |
| 6 | 6 | 66 | 200 | Green | Red | 9 | F | 12 | Tennis |
| 7 | 7 | 69 | 250 | Blue | Red | 10 | F | 12 | None |
| 8 | 8 | 54 | 122 | Blue | Brown | 5 | M | 9 | Basketball |
| 9 | 9 | 57 | 101 | Blue | Brown | 6 | F | 12 | Basketball |
| 10 | 10 | 58 | 178 | Brown | Black | 4 | F | 10 | Track |
| 11 | 11 | 59 | 199 | Hazel | Blond | 8 | F | 10 | Track |
| 12 | 12 | 59 | 260 | Green | Black | 9 | F | 9 | Track |
| 13 | 13 | 60 | 145 | Blue | Brown | 10 | M | 11 | None |
| 14 | 14 | 60 | 158 | Brown | Blond | 11 | M | 10 | Basketball |
| 15 | 15 | 57 | 197 | Brown | Black | 12 | M | 11 | None |
| 16 | 16 | 66 | 126 | Blue | Red | 6 | F | 10 | Track |
| 17 | 17 | 67 | 278 | Green | Brown | 5 | F | 12 | Track |
| 18 | 18 | 68 | 225 | Hazel | Black | 9 | F | 10 | Track |
| 19 | 19 | 69 | 103 | Blue | Blond | 7 | M | 11 | Basketball |
| 20 | 20 | 70 | 111 | Blue | Red | 5 | M | 10 | None |
| 21 | 21 | NA | NA | NA | NA | NA | M | 9 | Tennis |
| 22 | 22 | NA | NA | NA | NA | NA | M | 11 | Basketball |
| 23 | 23 | NA | NA | NA | NA | NA | M | 10 | Basketball |
| 24 | 24 | NA | NA | NA | NA | NA | M | 11 | None |
| 25 | 25 | NA | NA | NA | NA | NA | M | 11 | Basketball |

Showing 1 to 25 of 25 entries

6. Install and load the `dplyr` package, if you have not done either of these already:

```
install.packages("dplyr") library(dplyr)
```

7. Create `students_right_join`, performing another right join, but this time using the `dplyr` join methods. Check the dimensions to verify the number of students' information in the joined dataset:

```
students_right_join <- right_join(students, students2, by = "ID")
dim(students_right_join)
```

8. Create `students_anti_join` similarly and check the dimensions. Based on the preceding table, is the output what you expected?

```
students_anti_join <- anti_join(students, students2, by = "ID")
dim(students_anti_join)
```

9. If the by variables are named the same things, you can actually do both merges and joins without specifying a by variable:

```
students_merge_noby <- merge(students, students2)
students_join_noby <- right_join(students, students2)
```

10. Rename the `ID` variable on students to be called `StudentID`. Now, merge and join the data using the slightly different by variable names to see how powerful merge and join functions truly are:

```
colnames(students)[6] <- "StudentID"
students_merge_diff <- merge(students, students2, by.x =
"StudentID", by.y = "ID")
students_join_diff <- right_join(students, students2, by =
c("StudentID" = "ID"))
```

**Output**: The following is the `students` dataset as an output:

```
Classes 'tbl_df', 'tbl' and 'data.frame': 20 obs. of 6 variables: $
Height_inches : int 65 55 60 61 62 66 69 54 57 58 ... $ Weight_lbs : int
120 135 166 154 189 200 250 122 101 178 ... $ EyeColor : chr "Blue" "Brown"
"Hazel" "Brown" ... $ HairColor : chr "Brown" "Blond" "Black" "Brown" ... $
USMensShoeSize: int 9 5 6 7 8 9 10 5 6 4 ... $ ID : int 1 2 3 4 5 6 7 8 9
10 ...
```

The following is the `students2` dataset as an output:

```
'data.frame': 25 obs. of 4 variables: $ ID : int 1 2 3 4 5 6 7 8 9 10 ... $
Gender: Factor w/ 2 levels "F","M": 1 1 1 1 1 1 1 1 1 2 ... $ Grade : num
10 10 9 10 12 9 12 12 11 10 ... $ Sport : Factor w/ 4 levels
"Basketball","None",..: 4 3 3 1 1 4 4 3 4 3 ... 4. [1] 20 9 5. [1] 25 9 7.
[1] 25 9 8. [1] 0 6 9b. Joining, by = "ID"
```

One commonality you may have noticed is that for both `merge()` and the `*_joins()` functions from `dplyr` is that you enter a by variable to merge or join on. If you don't, in general, both types of functions will be able to detect what to join on as long as the variables are named the same thing. If you're in a situation where the variables are not named the same thing (which is common!), you'll have some trouble. In that case, where the by variables are named two different things, you will have to specify the two different names so that the functions know what to do, as you did in the example.

It's not uncommon in data science to have to merge or join multiple datasets when you work with data in R. While you're learning, you may encounter a lot of datasets that are already joined, but the reality of data work is that you often have to take data from disparate sources and combine it.

# Activity: Merging and Joining Data

**Scenario**

You work at a school, where you've been tasked with updating the data for one of the high school English classes. Use your merging and joining skills to get the data in the final state your boss requires.

**Aim**

To practice merging and joining datasets. Prerequisites Make sure that R and RStudio are installed on your machine.

**Steps for Completion**

1. Re-import the `students` dataset from the repository on GitHub. The best way to do this is by using the following code:

   ```
   read_csv("https://github.com/TrainingByPackt/R-Programming-Fundamen
   tals/blob/master/lesson1/students.csv")
   ```

To use this code, you have to load the `readr` package!

Add an `id` variable to students equal to the number of rows of students.

2. Navigate to `lesson3_activityC2.R` on GitHub to get the code you need to create the second and third students datasets.

3. Merge the three datasets until you arrive at one with 16 rows and 12 variables:

   The variables should be in the following order: `StudentID`, `Height_inches`, `Weight_lbs`, `EyeColor`, `HairColor`, `USMensShoeSize`, `Gender`, `Grade`, `Sport`, `HomeroomTeacher`, `ACTScore`, `CollegePlans`.

4. Join the datasets until you arrive at one with 25 rows and 12 variables:

   The variables should be in the following order: `Height_inches`, `Weight_lbs`, `EyeColor`, `HairColor`, `USMensShoeSize`, `StudentID`, `HomeroomTeacher`, `ACTScore`, `CollegePlans`, `Gender`, `Grade`, `Sport`.

# Summary

Data management is a crucial skill needed for working with data in R, and we have covered many of the basics in this chapter. One thing to keep in mind is that there is no prescribed order in which to conduct data management, cleaning, and data visualization. Rather, it will be an iterative process that likely won't end, even if you continue with your data and perform data analysis projects. You will probably run across more questions about your data if you use it to build statistical models.

This book was hopefully only the beginning of your R pro. It has taken you through variable types, basic flow control, data import and export, data visualization with base plots and ggplot2, summarizing and aggregating data, plus joins and merging to help you build a foundation for how to use R to work with data. However, the Comprehensive R Archive Network, or CRAN, the largest repository of R packages available for download, contains more than 10,000 R packages built by R users to accomplish many different tasks with R. There are even more packages available on GitHub, Bioconductor, and other places online. Chances are, if you're looking to do it in R, someone has built a package that will at least get you started.

# Solutions

This section contains the worked-out answers for the activities present in each lesson. Note that in case of descriptive questions, your answers might not match the ones provided in this section completely. As long as the essence of the answers remain the same, you can consider them correct.

# Chapter 1: Introduction to R

The following are the activity solutions for this chapter.

## Activity: Installing the Tidyverse Packages

1.  Open the project we created in the subtopic *Using R and RStudio* called `IntroToDSwRCourse`. You will see the following screen:

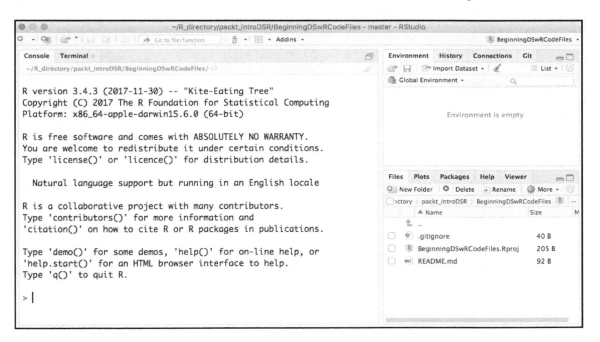

2. Create another new R script, using either **File** | **New File** | **R Script**, or by clicking the top - left button that looks like a piece of white paper with a green arrow over it, and selecting **R Script**.

3. In the new script, type `install.packages("tidyverse")` and click **Run**, or use *Ctrl + Enter*. You should now see something along the lines of the following screenshot in the console. Also, if you scroll through the packages in the lower right corner, Tidyverse will now be listed among them:

```
> install.packages("tidyverse")
also installing the dependency 'haven'

trying URL 'https://cran.rstudio.com/bin/macosx/el-capitan/contrib/3.4/haven_1.1.1
.tgz'
Content type 'application/x-gzip' length 839173 bytes (819 KB)
==================================================
downloaded 819 KB

trying URL 'https://cran.rstudio.com/bin/macosx/el-capitan/contrib/3.4/tidyverse_1
.2.1.tgz'
Content type 'application/x-gzip' length 77756 bytes (75 KB)
==================================================
downloaded 75 KB


The downloaded binary packages are in

/var/folders/pn/bbp_y4nd58l5rjtnqj9yj0_40000gn/T//RtmpSUrCXn/downloaded_packages
>
```

4. The graphical user interface lists the packages that are installed on your machine in the **Packages** tab, as follows:

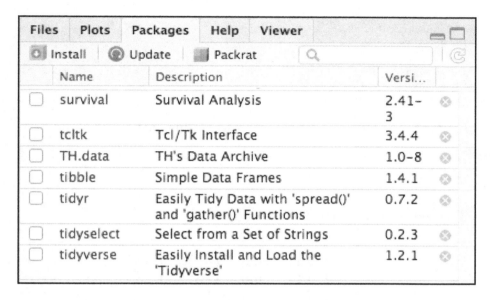

5. Save this R script with the name `install_packages`. You can save R scripts by either navigating to **File | Save As** or by hitting *Ctrl + S* (or *cmd + S*, on a macOS). It is now saved in your working directory as `install_packages.R`.

6. Load the `ggplot2` package with the code `library(ggplot2)`. `ggplot2` is a package contained in the `tidyverse` set of packages.

7. Load the `msleep` dataset by using `data("msleep")`. Examine the variables in this dataset by using `str(msleep)`.

8. Save a copy of the global environment to the working directory.

When you install a package, installation-related text will print to your console in red. This doesn't mean that something has gone wrong! Watch out for the words error or warning. If neither appear, the installation is fine, despite the red text.

# Activity: Identifying Variable Classes and Types

**Code**:

```
class("John Smith")
typeof("John Smith")
...
class(as.Date("02-03-28"))
typeof(as.Date("02-03-28"))
```

 Go to https://goo.gl/qmo4UR to access this code.

**Output**:

The preceding code provides the following output:

```
[1] "character"
[1] "character"
[1] "numeric"
[1] "double"
[1] "integer"
[1] "integer"
[1] "numeric"
[1] "double"
[1] "numeric"
[1] "double"
[1] "character"
[1] "character"
[1] "Date"
[1] "double"
```

Thus, the table provided in this scenario can be filed in as follows:

| Variable | Class | Type |
|---|---|---|
| `"John Smith"` | character | character |
| `16` | numeric | double |
| `10L` | integer | integer |
| `3.92` | numeric | double |
| `-10` | numeric | double |
| `"03-28-02"` | character | character |
| `as.Date("02-03-28")` | Date | double |

# Activity: Creating Vectors, Lists, Matrices, and Dataframes

1. Create vectors using the following code:

```
vec1 <- c(1:10)
vec2 <- c(LETTERS)
vec3 <- c(1, "A", 2, "B", 3, "C", 4, "D")
```

2. Create lists using the following code:

```
list1 <- list(1:10)
list2 <- list(LETTERS)
list3 <- list(list("popcorn", "kale"), list("the Blacklist", "This
is Us", "The X-Files"), list("run", "listen to podcasts", "paint my
nails", "learn data science"))
```

3. When you've created the lists, go and look in the environment and hit **View** to see the third list. Expand each list in the list of lists to see your answers and the types, as shown in the following screenshot:

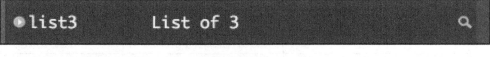

| Name | Type | Value |
|------|------|-------|
| list3 | list [3] | List of length 3 |
| [[1]] | list [2] | List of length 2 |
| [[1]] | character [1] | 'popcorn' |
| [[2]] | character [1] | 'kale' |
| [[2]] | list [3] | List of length 3 |
| [[1]] | character [1] | 'the Blacklist' |
| [[2]] | character [1] | 'This is Us' |
| [[3]] | character [1] | 'The X-Files' |
| [[3]] | list [4] | List of length 4 |
| [[1]] | character [1] | 'run' |
| [[2]] | character [1] | 'listen to podcasts' |
| [[3]] | character [1] | 'paint my nails' |
| [[4]] | character [1] | 'learn data science' |

4. Create matrices using the following code:
   1. Use `cbind()` to combine the vector 1:10 and the vector A:Z:

   ```
   matrix1 <- cbind(vec1, vec2)
   ```

   2. Use the following code to combine these two into a matrix, albeit one that will be coerced to character type:

   ```
   matrix_solution <-cbind(vec1, vec2[1:10])
   ```

5. Create dataframes using the following code:

```
df1 <- as.data.frame(matrix_solution)
df2 <- rbind.data.frame(c(1:5), c(6:10), c(11:15), c(16:20),
c(21:25))
names(df2) <- c("one", "two", "three", "four", "five")
```

# Activity: Building Basic Loops

The code we have developed thus far is as follows:

```
#load datasets
data("iris")
data("ChickWeight")

# if
var <- 100

  if((var/5) >= 25){
    print("Big number")
  }
...
  }else{
    Diet4 <- rbind(Diet4, ChickWeight[chick,])
  }
}
```

 Go to `https://goo.gl/rCMPpF` to access this code.

# Activity: Exporting and Importing the mtcars Dataset

1. Open a new R Script and save it as a file called `lesson1_activityD.R`.
2. Load the `datasets` library, and then the `mtcars` dataset with the following code:

```
library(datasets)
data("mtcars")
```

3. View `mtcars` with the `str()` function to see the data names, types, and how many observations and variables there are. The code will be as follows:

   ```
   str(mtcars)
   ```

4. Create a variable called `hpcyl`, which is equal to the horsepower per cylinders of each car as follows:

   ```
   mtcars$hpcyl <- mtcars$hp/mtcars$cyl
   ```

5. Write `mtcars` into a `.csv` file called `mtcars_out.csv`. If you have a program installed that will allow it, open it on your computer and verify that the `hpcyl` variable is inside. The code will be as follows:

   ```
   write.csv(mtcars, "mtcars_out.csv")
   ```

6. Read the dataset back in and call it `mtcars_in` by using `read.csv()`. The code will be as follows:

   ```
   mtcars_in <- read.csv("mtcars_out.csv")
   ```

# Activity: Exploring the Introduction to dplyr Vignette

**Code:**

```
...
filter(flights, month == 1, day == 1)
flights[flights$month == 1 & flights$day == 1, ]
#arrange
arrange(flights, year, month, day)
arrange(flights, desc(arr_delay))
#select
select(flights, year, month, day)
select(flights, year:day)
select(flights, -(year:day))
...
```

 Go to `https://goo.gl/eHbzjN` to access this code.

# Chapter 2: Data Visualization and Graphics

The following are the activity solutions for this chapter.

## Activity: Recreating Plots with Base Plot Methods

The following code can be used to load the `datasets` library:

```
library(datasets)
install.packages("ggplot2")
library(ggplot2)
```

The following code can be used to load the data:

```
data("iris")
data("mpg")
```

The following code can be used to create a scatterplot to plot petal width without an axis label:

```
plot(iris$Petal.Width)
```

The following code can be used to create a scatterplot to plot petal width without axis labels:

```
plot(iris$Petal.Width, iris$Petal.Length,
    main = "Petal Length vs. Petal Width",
    xlab = "Petal Width",
    ylab = "Petal Length")
```

The following code can be used to create scatterplots in *1x2* grids to plot petal length and width with axis labels:

```
par(mfrow = c(1,2))
plot(iris$Petal.Width, iris$Petal.Length,
    xlab = "Petal Width",
    ylab = "Petal Length")
plot(iris$Sepal.Width, iris$Sepal.Length,
    xlab = "Sepal Width",
    ylab = "Sepal Length")
dev.off()
```

The following code can be used to create a histogram using `mtcars` data to plot the number of cylinders in the color blue:

```
plot(as.factor(mpg$cyl),
    col = "blue",
    xlab = "# of cylinders")
```

# Activity: Recreating Plots Using ggplot2

The following code can be used to load the `datasets` library:

```
library(ggplot2)
```

The following code can be used to create a histogram to plot petal width:

```
ggplot(iris, aes(Petal.Width)) + geom_histogram(binwidth = 0.5)
```

The following code can be used to create a scatterplot to plot petal length and width:

```
ggplot(iris, aes(Petal.Width, Petal.Length)) + geom_point()
```

The following code can be used to create a boxplot to plot petal length and the `Species` factor variable:

```
ggplot(iris, aes(as.factor(Species), Petal.Width)) + geom_boxplot()
```

The following code can be used to create a bar chart using the `gear` variable of the `mtcars` dataset:

```
ggplot(mtcars, aes(gear)) + geom_bar()
```

# Activity: Utilizing ggplot2 Aesthetics

The following code is used to recreate the various plots using the mpg and diamonds datasets:

```
ggplot(mpg, aes(class)) + geom_bar(fill = "purple")

ggplot(mpg, aes(class, fill = as.factor(drv))) + geom_bar(position = "fill")

#scatter plot
ggplot(diamonds, aes(carat, price, col = cut)) + geom_point(alpha = 0.4)

ggplot(diamonds, aes(carat, price)) + geom_point(shape = 6, alpha = 0.3)
```

# Chapter 3: Data Management

The following are the activity solutions for this chapter.

# Activity: Creating and Manipulating Factor Variables

Use the following code to load the datasets library:

```
library(datasets)
```

Use the following code to load the diamonds dataset:

```
data("diamonds")
```

The function str() can be used to examine the diamonds dataset as follows:

```
str(diamonds)
```

We understand that there are three factors of ordered type as we examine the diamonds dataset. To identify the class of those factors, we can use the function class() as follows:

```
class(diamonds$cut)
class(diamonds$color)
class(diamonds$clarity)
```

The following code can be used to load the `midwest` dataset:

```
data("midwest")
```

The `str()` function can be used to examine the `midwest` dataset as follows:

```
str(midwest)
```

The following code can be used to convert the character variables into factor variables using the `apply()` method for changing many variables at once:

```
to.factor <- c("county", "state", "category")
midwest[,to.factor] <- data.frame(apply(midwest[,to.factor], 2, as.factor))
```

We can confirm if the character variables have been converted into the factor variable using the `str()` method, as follows:

```
str(midwest)
```

# Activity: Creating Data Summarization Tables

The following is the code we need to execute to accomplish the activity:

```
library(dplyr)
library(datasets)
#below:
table(diamonds$clarity)
table(diamonds$clarity, diamonds$color)
diamonds %>% group_by(clarity) %>% summarise(median(depth))
```

# Activity: Implementing Data Summary

The following code can be used to load the `mtcars` dataset and examine it:

```
data("mtcars")
str(mtcars)
```

Use the following code to summarize all the variables in the mtcars dataset that are not categorical, and find the mean and variance of each:

```
apply(mtcars[,-c(2,10,11)], 2, function(x) c(mean(x), var(x)))

diamonds %>% group_by(color, clarity) %>% summarise(median(price))
diamonds %>% filter(color != "D" & color != "H") %>% group_
by(color) %>% summarise(median(depth))
```

# Activity: Demonstrating Splitting and Combining Data

1. Load the mtcars dataset using the following code:

```
install.packages("datasets")
library(datasets)
data("mtcars")
```

Split the data by the cyl variable as follows:

```
mtcars_split <- split(mtcars, mtcars$cyl)
```

Create one dataset for each level of cyl using the following code:

```
mtcars_4 <- mtcars_split[[1]]
mtcars_6 <- mtcars_split[[2]]
mtcars_8 <- mtcars_split[[3]]
```

Recreate mtcars by unsplitting the split version of the data as follows:

```
mtcars_unsplit <- unsplit(mtcars_split, mtcars$cyl)
```

2. Combine the data using the following code:

```
l1 <- letters[1:4]
l2 <- letters[5:8]
l3 <- letters[9:12]
l4 <- letters[13:16]
l5 <- letters[17:20]
```

Create the following datasets letters1 and letters2 as follows:

```
letters1 <- rbind.data.frame(l1, l2, l3, l4, l5)
letters2 <- cbind.data.frame(l1, l2, l3, l4, l5)
```

# Activity: Merging and Joining Data

The following is the code we need to execute to accomplish the activity:

```
library(readr)
students <-
read_csv("https://github.com/TrainingByPackt/R-Programming-Fundamentals/blo
b/master/lesson1/students.csv")
students$StudentID <- seq(1:nrow(students))

students2 <- data.frame("ID" = seq(1:25),
                        "Gender" = sample(c("M","F"), size = 25, replace =
TRUE),
                        "Grade" = sample(c(9,10,11,12), size = 25, replace
= TRUE),
                        "Sport" = sample(c("Basketball", "Tennis", "Track",
"None"), size = 25, replace = TRUE))

str(students2)
```

Go to `https://goo.gl/ST87z5` to access this code.

# Other Books You May Enjoy

If you enjoyed this book, you may be interested in these other books by Packt:

**Hands-On Data Science and Python Machine Learning**
Frank Kane

ISBN: 978-1-78728-074-8

- Learn how to clean your data and ready it for analysis
- Implement the popular clustering and regression methods in Python
- Train efficient machine learning models using decision trees and random forests
- Visualize the results of your analysis using Python's Matplotlib library
- Use Apache Spark's MLlib package to perform machine learning on large datasets

**Kali Linux Cookbook - Second Edition**
Corey P. Schultz, Bob Perciaccante

ISBN: 978-1-78439-030-3

- Acquire the key skills of ethical hacking to perform penetration testing
- Learn how to perform network reconnaissance
- Discover vulnerabilities in hosts
- Attack vulnerabilities to take control of workstations and servers
- Understand password cracking to bypass security
- Learn how to hack into wireless networks
- Attack web and database servers to exfiltrate data
- Obfuscate your command and control connections to avoid firewall and IPS detection

# Leave a Review - Let Other Readers Know What You Think

Please share your thoughts on this book with others by leaving a review on the site that you bought it from. If you purchased the book from Amazon, please leave us an honest review on this book's Amazon page. This is vital so that other potential readers can see and use your unbiased opinion to make purchasing decisions, we can understand what our customers think about our products, and our authors can see your feedback on the title that they have worked with Packt to create. It will only take a few minutes of your time, but is valuable to other potential customers, our authors, and Packt. Thank you!

# Index

Made in the USA
Columbia, SC
04 August 2019